LIFE AFTER DETOUR

LIFE AFTER DETOUR

First Hand Advice to Empower Teen Parents

DEANNA JONES

J. Merrill
PUBLISHING

ISBN: 978-1-950719-38-9 (Paperback)
ISBN: 978-1-950719-39-6 (eBook)

Library of Congress Control Number: 2020909270

First printing edition 2020.

J Merrill Publishing, Inc.

434 Hillpine Drive

Columbus, OH 43207

www.JMerrillPublishingInc.com

CONTENTS

FOREWORD

Deanna Jones is the embodiment of perseverance. Deanna is the exertion of realness and the product of having faith through all things. Deanna is my sister, mentor, and friend. I look up to her and admire her, not just for her accomplishments, but for everything she has overcome to get here.

When I first met Deanna 14 years ago, I never would have imagined our relationship would become what it is. I was accepted into the family with open arms and loved just the same as a blood sister. I didn't know what true love from family felt like, and once I did, I was comforted. I knew from that day forward that this was my family, and they loved my children and me equally the same.

As Deanna shares her story and supports the transition of teens to see the good in all situations, I embrace her story and reflect on my own. Both of us being teen mothers in a world where our behavior for our age was ostracized and criticized. I look at the reality of how we should have been treated. We should have been educated and validated on the principles of motherhood and shown how to love our children —not partaking in conversations that discuss the aversion of our acts of passion. I am excited about the things to come and my sisters' devotion toward teen mothers everywhere to know they are not alone.

This book is a guide to teens around the world. A documentation of what to really expect when you're expecting and how a teen mom can persevere in certain situations. I appreciate the perspective this book gives. I consider the amount of confidence this would have given me when I began my journey into motherhood. This book provides advice and direction to teens who become mothers overnight. A realistic account from someone who has experienced the ups and downs of teenage emotion mixed with motherly hormones. Teen mothers everywhere need support and understanding, and Deanna is bringing that to life with her story. Enjoy!

- Dasha Tate, Faithful Birth Doula

PREFACE

Thank you for purchasing my book. I hope that as it blesses you that you share how it has blessed you with others who may benefit from it. From the onset, I want to share that this book is not written to fit in with the other "parenting" books. There are so many books, journals, and articles offering information about every aspect of pregnancy. From conception to delivery and points of development in between, there is so much information regarding you and baby. What I found is there is a wealth of unwritten information that is beneficial. It is the information you get from an older sister, an aunt, or a seasoned mother. It is the transparency about the things or feelings that we have that you can only share if asked, but you don't readily share. This was the entire desire of me writing this book. Granted, we know that there are things that we've heard before or things that have you going, "why didn't I think of that"? IF you happen to have an a-ha moment, then my mission has been accomplished.

As a former teenage mother, I have written this book from that perspective. I do think that fathers are essential and in no way intend to give the impression that fathers do not matter. They absolutely do. I want to be genuine and include fathers as much as I can when sharing this advice. Fathers have rights, and my advice to any father would be to know your rights! In anything in this life, there is a "why,"; the reason that you are doing a thing. Allow me to share with you, the reader, my "why" for writing this book. My "why" is simple. I want you, the reader, to gain information and insight that you may not have but need. I want you to have encouragement and a different point of view to assist you in navigating this parenting journey! I sincerely hope you find benefit in this advice that I wish I had as I began my journey as a new parent.

Inside you will find chapters with subjects ranging from the time I got pregnant to relationships and as well as various aspects of the parenting experience. Given that this book is geared toward teenage/young adult parents, the subject matter tends to be aimed at that sect of the population. However, I believe the information and stories I share can be helpful to older readers as well.

I want to share one thing with you as you begin reading. Throughout this book, I utilize lists to achieve my goals. In creating these lists, I realize there are foundational skills that are essential in planning out your lists; the ability to analyze and prioritize. I do take you through some rationale in each chapter about crafting why I am crafting the list of recommendations. Still, in general, I wanted to expound on that here. The first thing I do is to analyze the most immediate goal that I want to accomplish. Next, I identify the first thing I need to do or attain to achieve that goal. Lastly, I look for barriers to achieving that goal so that I can find remedies to remove those barriers. Finally, it is important to note that you may have a different set of things to do for each goal. For instance, opening a business will have a different set of tasks to complete then deciding to enroll in college. You can make an overall order of goals you want to accomplish and then go after each target using the aforementioned simple outline.

Additionally, identify the timeframe for what is an Immediate, short-term, and long-term goal. For me, Immediate is within 30 to 60 days. Short-term is within a 3-6-month period. Long-term is a year to three years. It should be noted that in all honesty, these can be changed as you need or want to change them. This is just a guide to get your mind going. With the goals, you must WRITE THEM DOWN. Put them where you constantly see them to ensure they are at the front of your mind when planning and going about your life. Focus on one goal at a time when possible!

My sincere hope is that I can encourage you wherever you find yourself in your pregnancy or on your journey of parenthood. I pray within the sharing of lessons that I have learned, you as the reader will gain something. Whether it helps you in a moment of weakness, clarifies things in a moment of darkness, or can uplift you when you are down on yourself. Parenting is a process and a journey. Thank you for taking me along.

Deanna.

DAG! THAT WAS A POSITIVE TEST
☹ WHAT WILL HAPPEN NOW?

I remember very vividly where I was when I discovered I was pregnant. The father and I were out at a local hang out. It was a very beautiful day. I just wasn't feeling right. In my heart, I knew I was pregnant, but I needed a test. I needed to know for sure. I couldn't go to the doctor because I was not ready to tell my parents. I expected my mother to flat out kill me as she had stated that she would kill any of her children if they had sex. I didn't expect a violent reaction from my father, but I did expect him to be apathetic. I couldn't be sure what WOULD happen, but I knew what COULD not happen...and that was my parents knowing at this time.

I remember telling my child's father to buy a test. He had just bought me lunch and some shoes, and he was broke. Of course, that did not stop him. He stole one and escorted me into the bathroom. That bathroom was grungy and dirty with walls the color of rotten mustard. The stench of stale urine greeted us as soon as we entered the bathroom, and yes, he escorted me into the bathroom. I took the test and waited in sickening expectation, then the confirmation. I was pregnant. We stared at each other scared and goofy. Suddenly the clouds did not seem so fluffy. We drove home in silence, both allowing our minds to swirl in our individual heads. The day had lost its luster for me at the realization that my life would never be the same.

I was feeling so many emotions! I had just begun to set up my next steps for my life. I didn't even want kids. Yes, that's right. This mother with three children here did not want kids. I planned to get my tubes tied as soon as I was 18. I was taking track and field more seriously. I planned on breaking up with my children's father. I had lined up a job at Kroger and prepared to save money to leave Ohio to live my best my life only to find out now all of that had to stop because I was pregnant. I was a great student who had just gotten a job at Kroger's. I was on the track team again and began to take great interest in my future. I planned to move far away and to live a curious life. My ambitions and goals were lofty and variable but completely attainable. I was excited about my life without children.

The life that I had lived, the abuses I had suffered, and the things that I had cemented my resolve not to raise children in this world. Additionally, I was "selfish," or so I was often told. I guess by definition, that was true. I had begun to put myself first, and I felt that I had earned that right. I had spent a lot of my life caring for my younger brother and sister. I was my mom's right-hand man. I was okay with that because I loved her and my siblings even though they got on my nerves. I knew once I got out of the house? I was done. I was done being a parent. Now here I was a parent. I felt like my life had come to an abrupt end when I just had begun to live! I was finding out what I liked to do and what I was good at. As a 14-year-old, I was a freshman in high school. I had friends at every stratum in school (the popular kids, the plastics, the average kids, the bad kids, and outcasts), but I was still alone. I was beginning to navigate through all of that, figuring out how to fit in. Of course, I learned to fit in. I had to just do me.

I scolded myself beyond compare. I then grew depressed. I could not figure out what I was going to do! The thing about me is, I cannot stay down long. I gratefully knew there was no victory in cutting myself down. There was no overcoming in undercutting myself. Granted, this obstacle that I now had to overcome was created of my own doing. I grew more determined to succeed as more people told me that I was going to be a statistic or as a high school dropout. I shouldn't even dream of attending college! I had to set aside this, and all of the other foolishness people spoke into my life. I was called "fast" and other names. I was shamed, and so were my parents with people saying all of these things about me, friends, and family alike. The applied names and labels; trying to tell me and the world who or what I was. What was I, though? My baby and I? Winners. We are going to win. In my mind, all I could think was, "watch this."

Crash. Before you know it? I had begun to believe what was being said to me. It began to be what I was saying to myself. So once again, I found myself picking myself up. Again. And that was okay. I found myself in this posture often, the position of rising. I had to do it often and still have to do that to this day. That's okay. That's what victors do! Even as an overcomer, you will have down days, bad days, you'll be angry, you'll be sad, and there will be days you may not be able to put those feelings into words. And that's okay. Just keep fighting. Don't give up!

I am sure that as you are reading this, you can also remember where you were when you find out you were going to be a parent. I would imagine there were waves of emotions for you as there were for me. I was sincerely in my feelings. Those feelings went back and forth, up and down before crashing in my stomach.

I was not ready for what would happen when I disclosed my secret for various reasons. The primary reason was my mother. I'll explain why.

When it came to the sex talk, I just received one piece of instruction, "Bitch, don't do it." My mother always stated that she would kill me. This was often peppered with various expletives and threats, so I believed her- I just thought I wouldn't be caught. I was curious, and I liked the power that I felt that I had. I reveled in the ability to consent, a right denied to me twice before. In any event, as a result of the threats mentioned above, I surmised that telling her was out. In fact, she only found out after realizing that I was not using sanitary products as often. (I hid them under my mattress while I figured out how to tell her). Granted, I was not the best liar. It remains a skill I'm sure I need to acquire.

Nevertheless, when my mother asked me directly, I could not lie. I confirmed what she dreaded; that at 15 years old, I was indeed carrying a child. I knew that I would disappoint my father. I felt guilty as the oldest child who was consistently supposed to be setting an example for my younger siblings, and now I'm pregnant. I felt like my life was completely over. There was no more me, no selfishness, and only MORE responsibility. Looking back, I am not sure what I expected from my parents once they found out, but what I did not expect was the word...abortion.

My mother said it so easily that it shocked me then, in a way that it does not now (that is a story for another day). To this day, it haunts met. It hurt me for a long time that this was even discussed for her first grandchild and so easily. Despite my rough upbringing, abuse, and overall exposure to trauma, my life (at this point) could go several ways. My parents were all abuzz with the endless possibilities until now. Once those words fell in the room, they ushered in the sense of sadness and desperation that I have not seen in my parents before, or since. In my mother's eyes, all of the opportunities and possibilities were quickly drifting away. She often told me that I could do anything I wanted. She told me there was only one other college graduate in my family, and I was to be the second. For my mother, the solution was easy...kill the baby, and all will be restored when in walks my father.

He stood 6'8" and could be very intimidating to others, but to me, he was just a tall teddy bear. My mother told him what was happening and when he turned to look at me, I wanted to disappear. Silence filled the room and space as my eyes drifted across the dark wooden paneling in the small front room. The lamp cast a dim light over the situation—such a fitting addition.

My mother ordered my father to talk some sense into me, which is exactly what I thought he was going to do, as she stared at me expectantly. Instead, he looked at me and asked me simply, "what do you want to do?" Immediately I stated, "Daddy, I want to keep it." He straightened his back and said, "Well, that's what we are going to do, but you WILL raise it." I nodded, in grateful agreeance. My mother tried later to force me to get an abortion, but I had done my homework and knew that she could not. Eventually, she came around and would be involved in the way a mother and grandmother should.

There is a lesson here, and it is this. It will be essential for you to do your homework. Do you want to keep this baby? Is an abortion right for you? Can you give your child the option of being adopted? How will this decision affect your life? You may have many weighing in, even instructing you or attempting to make you go the way they feel you should go. Realize they cannot force you to do anything. Bearing that in mind, any decision you will have to make will be one YOU and you ALONE will have to carry this child. Keeping that in mind, how much more will it be something YOU can live with? You may or may not have help, but they have the option of staying or leaving and helping or not. They also control what that help, and their presence looks like, regardless of your needs. Whatever decision you make will have to be an informed one. And it will have to be a decision independent of those people and circumstances around you.

You may lose friends as other parents fear your, ahem, "looseness" will affect their daughters or trap their sons. Family members may talk about both you and your parents. It will bother you, some more than others. Let me also parenthetically insert this here. For some reason, I did not expect people to talk about me to the degree they did. It was astonishing. Looking back, it still blows my mind.

It will be at this point that you will have to make another decision not to believe what is said about you. I know that I made a mistake in getting pregnant before I was ready. Very few people plan to have a baby at 15 years old, and those that do have not fully considered the repercussions of that decision. I want you to understand something. You cannot change the way people feel about you. You cannot change how they view you. What you can control is what you accept from them and what names you answer to (including the names you respond to and believe in your head).

The reality of it all is simple. If you have not done so at this point, you will certainly need to decide who you are and who you are not. Once you do, it needs to be settled and non-negotiable. Why? So, when you hear things said about you that are not true, negative, or defeating-you can immediately reject them, giving no place for them in your mind or your life. Knowing who you are empowers you and enables you to train anyone who comes into contact with you as to how to treat you.

Granted, I felt like I knew who I was, but this baby definitely challenged that. It gave me more of an opportunity to define who I was. I was not "fast." I was not a slut. This was not some grandiose plan to trap my son's father; regardless of this being a "choice" or not, you now find yourself as a parent. Although your child is not here yet, you have probably already discovered that you are responsible for that life! As such, you will need to do your homework!

Here's an excellent place to examine what you want for your life. Yes, you still have a life. Yes, you still get to live it. Now you just have to be more painful and more mindful to ensure that you have the life that you want. This is just a part of being an on-point woman or non-point man. You have to know what you want for yourself. You have to have your own goals you have to have your own ideas, and you have to have your own plan. You can get help with that plan, and you can get help setting up that plan or making that plan. But what you need to do is have an ironclad plan and goals for yourself to accomplish. This plan doesn't need to be significant, so don't make it harder than it has to be. You have to feel secure and confident in executing it. You can always add to it or amend it so that you can both know who you are and see where you are going so you can work this plan.

Even reading this, you may still feel like, Deanna, how am I supposed to do that? I still can't believe I'm pregnant; I'm still in denial. If you find yourself in denial at this point, that's okay. The reality of it is that once you decide to have this baby, you're no longer in denial. You may still be in a place of disbelief, but you are not in denial. Decide from this point on what you want for your life. Granted, this may change. And that's okay. Knowing what you want to do is freeing because it prevents you from focusing on things that do not need your attention.

So, you need to know do I want to go to college do I want to work. It's all about what you want to do.

Because you have to be forward-thinking to be successful, you can't be a loser. Just have an idea of what you want to do overall with your life. Then identify what you want for your pregnancy. Again, thinking that far ahead can be overwhelming, but even if you are just rolling around ideas, that's the start of building your foundation. You will need to know what you want for school, for your child, for the relationship with your parents, and for you. Figure out how to achieve it with the understanding that obstacles will arise. Remember to be honest. You cannot prepare for something if you do not have an accurate assessment of what you need to do.

Furthermore, things and plans will change! That is okay. Try to keep that in your mind so that you can adjust when the inevitable tide turns.

When I found out I was pregnant, I immediately went into planning mode. Having grown up rougher than some, I knew the importance of having a plan. I had identified what was most important to me; that was finishing high school and going on to college. Sitting here, I can remember how daunting a dream that was! I was 14, living in a dysfunctional family and home with little support, and pregnant. I put my plan into action and taking stock of what worked and what didn't.

How far along are you? Based on your answer, this will determine what your next course of action is. At the end of each chapter, I will provide you with a checklist to help point you in the right direction and focus those thoughts. When I am composing a list, I start with my goals. Next, I look at the best path to achieving that goal. Thirdly, I would look at obstacles and come up with a plan to remove those obstacles. Lastly, I would prioritize them with time-sensitive items at the top of the list. Also, if a task needs to be completed before another task, that goes on the top of the list. If something is at the bottom and does not get done on time, move that to the top of your next list. It's important to note that you don't have to finish your list as you have written it to write the next one. You can cross tasks that you have accomplished and make a new list with other things you have identified that you needed to do.

With these things in mind here is a checklist of things to do, or consider doing, based on how far along you are:

- If the father does not know, plan on how you are going to tell him and who will be present? If you are the father or parental family, how are you executing plans to be actively involved in your child's pregnancy and life? Conflict is not a reason to be absent from your child's life. Remember that. Conflict is not a reason to not financially and emotionally support your child.
- If your parents do not know, plan on how you are going to tell them and who will be present in the delivery room. As you complete both of these tasks, determine if you feel safe to tell your parents and the father of your child. If not, we need to identify support to ensure your safety at this point and going forward.
- Outline how your schooling will be impacted and how you plan to finish (and yes, you absolutely can and WILL finish). This may be something that requires a lot of work and planning. If so, that's okay. Be honest about where you are and what you need to finish school. Identify resources that can help you.
- Schedule a doctor's appointment
- Look and see if there is a community service for teenage parents.
- Contact your job and family services to see what benefits they may able to provide and what will be needed to start that process.
- Create a plan to take care of you! At this point, I would contact your local Doula agency or even an independent Doula. They can help you come up with a plan that will include your wishes about your care. Communicating your wishes, following doctor's orders, learning about your body, what you should/ should not eat, what helps you to de-stress,

what encourages you, and what builds you up! Whatever the plan, it should be something that you will realistically follow!

- Lastly, list out the ways that you can work with the other parent to help each other achieve a healthy and successful life for your child. Even it's just one thing, for now, that's okay! Start laying that foundation!

All of these tasks can be done with your parents. If you can use them, by all means, please do so. Parents are a wealth of information, as we will discuss later!

STUCK LIKE GLUE - BONDING AND ATTACHMENT

Writing this chapter, I am transported back to the months after I found out I was pregnant. It was very easy to stay disconnected from my child-until it wasn't. Yes, I was pregnant, but it didn't seem real, and I was disconnected from that reality. The reality was not where I lived. I was living in Denial until situations or things brought me closer to reality. Let me explain.

I was disconnected until I had to acknowledge that I could not eat blue cheese and seafood. It made me have to face facts. I am a mother. I am responsible for another person. Not only that, but I am also carrying a whole other person. I had to begin to face the fact that my son was not a hindrance or a burden but a whole human being. He was a blessing and was wholly dependent on me. Depending on me to take care of myself, and even be mindful of what I put in my body so that he could develop properly. I accepted this, and once I did, the shell had started to crack- I was becoming bonded to my baby. Little bit by little bit. I moved from the land of denial into the depths of my reality.

Looking back, I have a better idea of why there was such a block. I was in the sea of denial. Early on, I was still doing what I wanted. I was physically wrestling with my siblings and cousins, running for fun, and more. The more pregnant I grew, the less I was able to live in the land of denial. Suddenly the vastness of this was shrinking and began to plunge me deeper into reality as it steadily approached me. At first, it was easy to stay on the shores.

At month 2, I wasn't showing. No major changes had occurred in my body. I was standing firm on the shore of denial. At month 5, I was showing, and it was no longer a secret of omission. Now those I interacted with realized I was pregnant and engaged me in that regard. The more my belly grew, the deeper I sank into the dark depths that was my reality. Friends began not to be friends anymore. Family members whispered loudly and judged louder than that...

At about seven months, I was now waist-deep in reality. It grew colder and more pervasive. My eyes scanned my life, and I knew it would never be the same. A friend of mine had a party six houses down from my house. I decided to have a little fun, and my mother encouraged this, stating it would be fun. I found my shoes. I went out of the house, worked past the stares, and the smart comments continued on the path to my friends' home. As I got closer, the music was louder, and children ran out of the house, and some were on the porch. I walked past them, shaking and tearful on the inside but cool as a cucumber outside. I stepped up to the door to be met by several pairs of eyes at the party. I will never forget the waterfall of the conversations almost immediately drying up. The music seemed obnoxiously louder in the absence of all other noise. My friend's mom tried to recover and invite me in, encouraging the other kids to do so as well. It was too late. My stone face and cool exterior were both cracked. I said nothing and attempted to smile politely so that I could leave. Lord knows if I was able to get the muscles of my face to comply. By the time I hit the sidewalk, the chatter had begun to fill the night air as tears filled my eyes.

I am not a crying person, but when I do, it's usually an emotional response. Even at that, I can usually keep it together, but I couldn't that night. I arrived home to be met by my mother. Having seen my eyes, she quickly sat up to read my face. She shook her head, waiting for an answer, but there was none. I sat on the couch and did something I had learned to do well by now; I cried silently.

That night may have been a blessing and a curse. My focus turned back to my child and me. I had begun to grow closer to him. I began speaking to him more, playing music for him, and at nine months, I was pretty bonded. It took nine months to feel bonded. It was nine months, and it was JUST now real for me! I was excited to meet my child; I was scared to face being a teen mom, and but I was now in love with my baby.

The thing is that if anyone had told me, "don't worry, you will grow to love your baby" or "You will attach to him or her. It's okay". I am not sure if I would have believed them. It certainly would have been helpful to know that I am was not alone. Through tears and disbelief, I would have listened, but I don't know if I would have felt that attachment. I felt terrible for not feeling bonded or attached as much as I thought I should be, but that was where I was. Yet, a little after 10:36 p.m., I saw him. His cry arrested my heart, and it stood still in awe only to be moved by a surge of love for him. Suddenly, I did not care that I wasn't going to prom or that my friends' parents were keeping their kids away from (like I had the plague. Mind you, they were more, ahem, advanced than I, but I digress). I no longer cared that I had not "lived" or would "miss out." I cared about my son. All I wanted was him. I wanted to love him and care for him to ensure that his needs are met. I loved him, and at that point, he was all that mattered. Everything was about him.

So why am I sharing this with you? For a very simple reason - in case you or a young parent, you may know, can identify with these feelings or concerns around bonding and attachment. That parent may not be attached, and "all of this" may not be real to them. That is okay, and it is normal. People adapt and begin this process at different points in your life. Let me affirm you and encourage you today. In case you are not feeling an attachment, please give it time. Allow yourself this time. Both to grow to naturally bond with your baby but to explore those feelings so that you can address them. You are still processing a lot!

Review the checklist in Chapter 1. IF any follow up is needed, plan to do that here and make you a mini-list for things do. Remember, anytime you talk to someone regarding business get their name and number

- Find ways that you and your baby can bond- techniques that work for you. I spoke to my baby. I played music for my son and read to him even in utero! Find out what works for you.
- Think about your future with your child. You will typically bond with your child naturally, so don't rush it. Once it becomes clear that you have a little person in your body, your maternal instincts kick in. Even if you feel like you don't have them, you will.
- If you still find yourself un-attached to your child later in the pregnancy, please seek a counselor and talk to your doctor. They may be able to offer hands-on assistance and help you figure out what your next steps should be.

✾　3　❧

A CHANGE IS GONNA COME... THE BABY IS ALMOST HERE, NOW WHAT?

Change is a part of life and a part of pregnancy. Thinking back to the months before my baby was due allows me to reflect on some of the things that I was feeling and enduring. My home life continued to be a daily roller coaster between the painful and the unimaginable on every front. Every time I tried to get a grip on a thing, there was a change. Most of which was out of my control. Before you knew it? My body joined the party, changing at will consistently. Depending on where you are in your pregnancy, you can feel one way at 8:00 a.m., and by 3:00 p.m., you may feel totally different. When you are told that your hormones are running rampant, this can affect your emotions. Know that you are indeed being told the truth. Let me share with you how I can state that in all honesty.

In 1997, I was pregnant with my daughter. I sincerely and wholeheartedly began to cry when the show Martin was canceled; yes, real tears. I was sad for a few days! Granted, the show was funny; but tears? No, my hormones had begun to ramp up, causing those tears to ramp up with it. On top of that, at that moment? I felt utterly alone, even in a house full of people, and my stress was ramping up. Let me explain.

·　·　·

My mother was on drugs, and my father had moved out. I had no adult support. My siblings did what they wanted and were younger, so they were, maybe even understandably so, no help there. I was in school, but I had since stopped due to the stress. Some of my "friends" were judgmental and were treating me differently. I remember parents not allowing their daughters to be friends with me as there was an assumption that I was fast or promiscuous, and neither was true. (In fact, to this day people assume that my children who are a year apart have different fathers because of the stereotypes of teen mothers). That perception was very common during that time. It was ironic that some of the young women who judged and defriended me were the very ones who were sexually active! There is no bitterness here! Let them think what they want. It has no power over you!

I now know that I suffered from depression, which grew worse and worse, the further I got along. I didn't have all that I needed for my baby, much less what I wanted and being in a nesting frame of mind, but with nothing to "nest" with made my depression worse. You may be experiencing that.

The American Pregnancy Organization defines nesting as, "This urge to clean and organize is known as nesting. Nesting during pregnancy is the overwhelming desire to get your home ready for your new baby". Nesting varies for each woman, both in degree and when it starts. At this time, you may be nesting. If you haven't yet, you will more than likely experience it, even in brevity. In short, nesting means you have a strong desire to prepare for your child. This can be manifested in decorating, buying tons of diapers or folding and refolding items you have to make things PERFECT for you and baby. For me, nesting was a luxury I did not have.

I cannot tell you when it started, but I remember the urge to straighten, clean, and prepare for my son's homecoming. My home was not ideal for bringing a child into, so this hampered my nesting desires a little. Can you blame me? My mom was on drugs, stealing from us, and fighting with her boyfriend. There were times when all I had to eat was cream-style corn for days because mom had sold our food banking on my father simply replacing it because his children were in the home. That worked until it didn't. Those times when it didn't work, it left my siblings, and I wonder what we would eat. Food was scarce, and so was the support. I had to contend with relatives talking about me, those in the community talking about me and dealing with open wounds and trauma while trying to straighten and prepare.

When I got pregnant with my son, I was 14 years old. Living at home and sharing a room with my younger sister. My son got a crib right before he was born. It was against a window in my room, partially blocking the utility closet that masqueraded as a closet for two. I had a makeshift nightstand that I put as much as I could get on there. The desire to nest could have been hampered due to not having much. Still, I digress because eventually, my mom did help me get the essentials, which I, in turn, put on my dresser. It was not ideal, but I was beyond being sad. I was so focused on being prepared for him. I rarely had time to focus on what I didn't have or how the nesting was meeting my expectations.

I had to focus. Focus on being the best mother I could be. I focused on the aspects of my nesting that I could complete. What did I have? I made it neat. I was grateful for it and set my sights on getting what I can when I can. I concluded that as long as I had somewhere to care for and feed him, we would be okay. I would do my best to do all that I could and the rest? I trusted God. If you don't believe in a higher other higher power, you still have the option to worry about what you can control. What is out of your control should not consume your time and mental space because worrying about that will not change your ability to affect them. It will not give you peace. Acceptance will! Accept that this is how it is now, but because it is temporal, it is subject to change!

Your baby is taking up more and more space leaving little for you, your lungs, your comfort, or your feelings! Your emotions will continue to ebb and flow, so prepare as you can. It is completely normal to be weepy or tired or "feeling some type of way." You may not be able to identify how you feel but try and find a healthy and safe way of expressing those feelings. Try and identify what you need to feel at ease right now. There will be a lot of things going through your mind.

Let me encourage you...that is okay! That is normal. Just be sure to get them out of your head, either in a journal or to a person. Try to be as logical as you can despite the (probable hormonal) propensity to be anything but.

With the baby coming and possibly feeling those nesting desires, changes felt in the body may be ramping up. Granted, each pregnancy is different. How your body may change may vary from the next, but it will change. It makes sense that it would! Your body has some major work to do to welcome your little bundle of joy, preparing to enter the world. The show Roseanne has an episode where one of the characters, Jackie, was asking how her baby was going to be born - physically. To Jackie, this was an impossible feat. In the scene, Jackie raised her shirt to show her pregnant belly. Her belly looked as if she had swallowed a large watermelon whole! She said, "how is this going to come out of this"? For all of the humor in the scene, it is a valid question. Did Jackie really have no idea? I venture to say she did understand to a degree, but knowing that didn't ease her acceptance of reality. Roseanne then replied, "Relax Jackie. These have been coming out of those for years. Muscles stretch, bones break..." While Roseanne's comedic delivery ensured this scene was hilarious, she's not wrong. Did you know that your pelvic symphysis softens to the point that a child can pass through? How amazing is that? Your body is working overtime to accomplish this amazing feat, so knowing those changes are coming. Getting informed about them and how to address them will help you. There are a few places you can get this information.

Read the books that talk about what is coming on. Most of them take you month to month and a little after delivery. Also, the print outs that the doctor gives you contain a wealth of information. Lastly, ask other moms any questions that you have. If they are a person who will have a conversation with you and you feel comfortable safely sharing with them, ask away! I encourage you to keep the information you get as a point of reference. This information is a blessing to have, but know that you may experience none of the things they have experienced. You might experience it all for what you learn, or you may experience it, but HOW you experience it may differ. The important thing is to try and prepare for these changes as much as you can.

At the time I was pregnant, I didn't have a lot of people to ask questions regarding the changes that my body was undergoing. I am grateful that I did have my mother. She was able to answer questions for me and was there as someone to ask questions after reading the book. Even if it was just me asking, "really"? She was there. For instance, when I was pregnant with my eldest son and in the last part of my last trimester, I was deemed high risk. Yes, because I was so young, but I had pre-eclampsia. According to American Pregnancy.org, pre-eclampsia is when you have high hypertension, protein in your blood, and high blood pressure. This is usually determined at week 20 or later. I was huge, and I was so uncomfortable. I was petrified as I was going to have my labor induced. My biggest fear was that I would die on the table. I remember lying on the floor with my mother, telling her I was afraid. I had begun to second guess my decision to keep this child. My mother, despite ALL of her flaws, was very loving at this moment. She comforted me and assured me that I would be safe. She admonished me in the Lord and told me that I would be safe. I typically can endure anything if I know it's coming. Even if that is not you, having a point of reference when you experience something new or different can be very helpful.

There is a phrase that applies here, and it is an ounce of preparation is worth more than a pound of cure. Loosely translated the preparation, in the beginning, will make your life easier than trying to fix something preventable in the end. For example, if I step on a nail, I will have to get it cleaned and possibly get a tetanus shot before bandaging it up so the wound could heal. If I wait, I run the risk of getting an infection. IF I then get an infection, I will have to take the preventative measures I just listed. Still, I will also have endured pain or discomfort that I could have avoided. Additionally, I would have extended how long I am dealing with that situation. If I had taken the time to do be proactive. So, what does preparation look like at this point? Here is a checklist for this chapter:

- If you are able, line up your support system now!
- If you haven't identified your ideal supports, that is okay. It will take more planning on your part. For instance, if you don't have someone to confide in when you are feeling down? Will journaling help? Can you go to a church? Is there a support group?
- Also, start looking to set up your mommy area! An extra firm pillow, some candles, and other favorite things to put in place for yourself. You will need it. If there is a hobby you enjoy, can you prepare for that now, so it is there to enjoy it when you need it?
- Identify what you still need or what you think you MIGHT need. No matter how little or insignificant it may seem to you, it may be something that could make a rough day just a little bit easier! Both you and baby win!
- Continue to locate familial and community supports that can assist you from this point and going forward.

4

FILLING YOUR SELF-CARE
TOOLBOX, HAVE PEACE.

I remember thinking, "if I always have my baby...why do I feel so alone? Is it bad that I "hate" my baby right now"? There was no one there to answer my question or to bounce those questions off of. One day my baby was inside my expanding belly, and the next, he/she was in my arms and needing something every moment of the day. The birth of my firstborn was a great time, but in an instant, the time and space to take care of myself vanished into thin air.

I was so overwhelmed. By the time I was 17, I was a teen mother of two children. Stairsteps mind you! My kids were one year, one month, and one day apart. Whew, what was I thinking? In the event, I was aging out of the foster care system and was alone. Looking back, I had a lot on my plate. I was separated from siblings, and my parents, told me I have to leave this apartment, I didn't have a high school diploma or a job and two infant children. No self-care at all! No taking time for myself or filling my cup. That honestly is the simplest form of self-care. For this book, let's define self-care as a dedicated and intentional act to ensure your needs are met. Self-care for you can look like staying up late to watch the late-night talk shows, long baths after the kids are in bed, or doing a crossword puzzle. It doesn't have to be as extravagant as a spa day or as lowly as a time out. If it's recharging and beneficial, it counts.

Depression was a bully, and for me, this was a losing game. Depression was already beating me; I was down. Then he called his friends anxiety and fear. Before you know it? It was over. I was down on the mat fighting to do the best I can to stay coherent and in the fight. I was doing the best I could, but it was a lot for me. As a person, I was lost. As a parent, I was lost and overwhelmed. I was overwhelmed with all of it. The preparation. The worrying for them. The screaming. The whining. The crying. These things are enough to make anyone go crazy. And I did to a degree. Moreover, I downed myself so much that any chance I had to overcome this depression was all but lost. From that point, I already suffered from depression, but in this situation, it worsened. I felt alone all the time. I can distinctly remember the first time I realized the importance of taking care of myself/ the impact of not taking care of myself.

There I sat in my apartment, quiet and unmoved. The casual observer would think I was sleeping with my eyes open, numb to the world around me. I can remember the feeling of the heavily used couch I was gifted when I moved into my aging out apartment. It had met its end long before finding its way to me. The couch was ribbed in the most awkward place. The pattern started monochromatic now donned what I hoped were water stains and vibrant flashes of various fruit juices from my babies. Affixed in the middle was I. My apartment was sparse, to say the least. There were no pictures on the walls. The only other place to sit was on the adjacent wall. It was a matching love seat that had the pillows strewn on the floor. They had become a bridge to some faraway land only inhabited by my children. Criss-cross applesauce I sat. My eyes glazed over from feeling every emotion but not knowing which one to settle on. I had cried as I did every day. I know the tears were more about the trauma I had yet to process and all of the dreams I did not know how to achieve, but yet, they still fell. Warm and thick, they landed on my round cheeks. Already saturated by now, my skin would not drink them in. So, they fell, finding their way onto my shirt. Due to my trauma, I had mastered the art of learning how to cry silently, and today was no exception.

Before I knew it? I was suffering from what I now know is psychosis. The Oxford Dictionary defines psychosis as "a severe mental disorder in which thought and emotions are so impaired that connection is lost with external reality." That was me. My depression had completely morphed into psychosis. I could stare for hours without a connection or memory by the end of the night. I felt like someone was living upstairs in my apartment. I had bargained with my "roommates." I stated to them, "just leave me and my children alone," and with that? I consented to allow "them" to stay in my home. I continued to stare as my children entertained themselves, and the roommates occupied their space. Finally, they took notice of my absence. Soon curious eyes found their way to me. Inquiries left their little lips, but my mind could not distinguish what they said. I fought to stay focused. My eyes found each other and then my children. Such concern for me. At that moment, I knew that something had to change.

The first thing I did was take a breath. I looked around at the apartment and decided I was not going to live in the discomfort of roommates. No longer would I barely pay my attention to my children because It was not fair for me. Although I struggled, I got my children bathed and in bed. I got the clothes picked up, and the house cleaned. It was 11 o'clock. All I wanted was to watch the news and be up alone. And that is what I did. It was the first time in a long time that I had something that was missing, peace.

I had no peace, and self-care was not a buzzword yet. There was no support for me then, so I did not have any concept of that. From then on, I committed to myself to be the best me I can be for me so that I can be the best mom for them. If there is an easy mutual benefit, then it's worth doing. It was hard because I had to figure out that I needed to do better, engaging in self-care and finding out the best place to start fixing it. It's sad to say that as a caseworker because, at this time, I was in foster care.

The agency that should have been there to help me was not. As a result, I was left to fend for myself as a parent and a young person. As a caseworker, I am grateful I never had a case where I was the perpetrator of abuse or neglect. I love my kids. They were the center of my world. I did not and would not abuse them. I wholeheartedly believe it was due to the times where I had to walk away from them for a minute. I had to leave them in the front room to sit in the kitchen at the table to have a moment alone. I am a firm believer in respecting my clients because I know that one decision made differently could result in my being in their shoes. I could be a statistic; beat by the barriers versus overcoming barriers. It is easy to see how a parent could end up on this boat. The proof is in the pudding. The statistics for child abuse are sobering. According to the CDC, 674,000 children suffered abuse or neglect in 2017 (https://www.cdc.gov/features/healthychildren/index.html). Other reasons contribute to children being abused or coming into care. Drugs, conflict, and more play a huge roll in the increase of children in care, but simple frustration is a contributing factor as well.

Most parents had uttered something disparaging about their child or being frustrated with their child when they had to remove themselves and take a moment. That is okay! You are human. You are allowed to be frustrated or need a break from your baby. Taking that moment helps to ensure that your child or children do not become part of the statistic.

I encourage it. It is a necessity. I was not able to get a break for my children for a long time. I did not trust anyone with my children except my cousin, and she's not always able to provide a break for me. Or she would come with me, and we will take my children out with us.

It's important to note that despite needing a break does not mean you RATIONALIZE leaving your child with individuals freely or lightly. Your friends and even your boyfriend/girlfriend may care about you. DO NOT ASSUME THE CARE THEY HAVE FOR YOU WILL CARRY OVER TO YOUR CHILD. This is why having support is vital. Use that support to get rest and engage in self-care when you can do so...safely. IF you don't have that support, you will have to strategic in resting as much as you can when you can. Can you plan to nap when they are napping? Can the children play nearby while you are cooking? Folding clothes? Is there anyone that you can trust to watch your children while you take a 30-minute walk? Is it possible to schedule quiet time or activities for your children so that you, too, can have some wind-down time? It may be only once a week for 15 minutes. That's okay. Start cultivating it those supports so you can be rested and cared for so that you can, in turn, care for your baby.

If you have the support to utilize a break for yourself, please use them. There are plenty of young mothers and fathers who wish they have that support. The reality of it is this is where self-care comes into play. Rest is so taken for granted in our society. It is not considered self-care until recently. Now whether you're on Facebook or Pinterest, people are talking about self-care. They are talking about rest. Rest is huge. You would be a different person in the morning if you had a fair amount of sleep versus someone who's had little to no sleep. The way that you respond to your babies will be different. The way that you respond to any irritation will be different. So, knowing that we have to assure that we have self-care. Let's talk about something a little difficult. I have found some new parents may feel some things that we would not want to admit they feel towards their child. I have heard of new parents feeling like they resent or even hate their child. I have to say that it is not a rare occurrence. Let me assure you that it is okay if you feel that way. I think that it is helpful and here's why. Because you are taking the time to say this is how I'm feeling. You are not abusing your child or neglecting your child as a result of the feelings you're having from your child crying. When you feel like these feelings are all you are feeling towards your child. I suggest discussing with your doctor or other resources to help you address these feelings to ensure that you are whole and that your child continues to be safe. What we don't want is for you to not safely address these feelings and result in having an open case or an injury to your child or worse.

As a veteran caseworker of over 11 years, I have had to work plenty of cases where the parent did not mean to hurt or even neglect their child. The father did not mean to say the things he said to his child. They were just "frustrated." Even in my early meetings with the parent, if I can see that they are stressed out, we stop there and address that fatigue. Whether it's a biological or a foster family, when I'd see a parent that had not been sleeping, eating well, or taken any time to relax away from the child, I started there. I would caution them that neglecting their selves does not help the situation, and it does not help the child. As a teen mom, I can definitely say that that was true. I mistakenly felt that I was not doing right by my kids by sending them to someone to care for them. Once I couldn't stop crying. I couldn't have a cohesive thought, and I knew I needed help.

I reached out to a service that my mother sent us to as children. It was called Turning Point. It was for parents to get a break, feeling upset, or they felt that they would hurt their children. It was a license for me to get a break, and to ensure my frustration did not overtake me. When I would call them, I will take them up there, and I would have the weekend to myself. It was unbelievable how much that helped me. It allowed us to engage in self-care and enjoy it. The seemingly smallest things were self-care. Waking up naturally, being able to go back to sleep, or doing a crossword puzzle freely. All of those things are so small, but at that time of my life, I would have had the ability to do them without Turning Point. After having it, I enjoyed seeing my children! I looked forward to playing with them and feeding them and providing for them after that break.

Self-care is also being committed to setting time aside for yourself and sticking to the plan. Regardless of what you do with that time, it needs to be set aside and honored the way you would any appointment for your child. My children took a nap every day even if they didn't go to sleep; it was "quiet time." They had to stay in their beds in their rooms. They usually would fall asleep, but sometimes they did not. The point is, when they were asleep, I would do what I wanted to do. Sometimes I will clean up, prepare snacks, or start dinner. Sometimes I simply just dozed off on the couch. Other times, I engaged in hobbies that I had set aside.

As they toddlers, my children became accustomed to quiet time and would usually just go to sleep next to me, or they were already sleep in their rooms. I definitely would not advise doing that before their time, but it's certainly something that I encouraged. In terms of lying down with your baby. When your babies are toddlers, and they're safe enough to lay down with you, sometimes you may need to nap with your baby. Next, once you have your schedule, stick to it. Don't use it all the time to go grocery shopping or to clean up. Your children can go with you to do both of those things, but they can't sit with you while you're watching an episode of Wild' N' Out or the show Power. Sleep in. Take time to get you a little me time in it is essential.

Take some time to identify some tools to utilize in your self-care toolbox. Supports from parents, family, friends. Planning some "me time" and still planning out your future. Even reading this, a parent may say, "Hate is such a strong word. I could never hate my baby!" Maybe not, but I have had a young mom ask me that and so I use that terminology here. No, you may not hate your baby, but feeling frustrated or being overwhelmed is highly probable. Knowing this can help you maintain your peace of mind and soul. Peace starts with a decision, and it is the prize at the end of every self-care session you set aside for yourself.

It will be soo easy to be distracted, sad, and in an uproar on the inside with no peace. Your child can feel that, whether he or she is in your belly or your arms. I can remember plenty of nights where I was nothing more than a container for a storm in my soul. I remember how my son would search my eyes looking for any indication that everything was okay despite him feeling how inherently sad mommy was. You will have those moments. An infant cannot tell you that they can feel your sadness or anger, but they can feel it. They will cry and not be easily comforted. How will that affect you? Furthermore, however, it impacts you will, in turn, influences the care and relationship you are having with your child. For me, my peace was obliterated. The lack of peace was apparent at different times of my life but in different ways.

As a teenager, my hair was falling out. As a young adult, I was so sleepy, but I could not sleep as my mind would not stop working. Now, when my peace is disturbed, I notice it in my mood, my ability to care, or concentrate. I have no motivation without peace, so I make it a point not to let my peace be disturbed in the first place. I have a rule in my life: There will be peace in my home! That sounds very simple, but it takes work at times to maintain that peace. To maintain that peace, it may require you to refuse entry into your home, thought life, or heart those people and situations that will disturb you. Sometimes it may take a difficult decision to say NO, but it is essential. Sometimes you will have to remove yourself from places, things, or people that at one point you found comfort in to ensure you have your peace. There was a person that was so close to me that I would have done anything for this person. After noticing certain things, it became clear that the season of this lifelong support had come to an end. I could have held on and tried to MAKE it work because of the history. The things I had been through with this person, or I can accept what it was NOW and choose to no longer let that person have a spot in my mental and emotional space. Peace is reciprocal. If you are pouring out peace and support but are not able to get it back, then you MUST be real about who or what you are pouring into. Identify what steps you need to take to restore peace and be committed to completing them. You as a woman matter. You as a father matter. You, as a person, matter! You deserve peace. You and your child will only benefit from it.

Peace is essential to ensure you have a healthy pregnancy, delivery, and a healthy baby! Peace means different things to different people. Be open to that! Also, know that things that may have brought you peace in the past may or may not work now. Try to focus on what works.

Peace is something that doesn't seem like a big deal. It doesn't seem like something you absolutely have to have. It may even be something that is a bit when moved. You might even be wondering why I would ask or speak to the subject of having peace. The reality of it is that piece is essential in your pregnancy. It is going to be necessary for your labor and delivery, and it's going to be vital in caring for yourself and your child after you give birth. The reality of it is that you have to be at peace throughout your life. This is an excellent time to start gaining those skills and putting them to work. Let me explain when I spoke about having peace during your pregnancy. It is essential because we know that stress has an impact on your child. If you're still carrying your child and planning on keeping this child, you want to make sure that your child is in the best position possible. You want your child to be healthy as they can be, right? So that requires you to start parenting now and be mindful of what you're putting into your child's spirit. What you're putting into your child's body because all of that affects your child's development. So if you're stressed and you don't have peace in your pregnancy, your child who's not even here yet will not have peace this will affect how they are doing in the womb why wouldn't you'd want to put your best foot forward and I think that you would.

It's important to practice having a peaceful state so that you're ready for a healthy delivery. During labor, when you're in that mode of blowing and breathing and counting your contractions, you definitely want to have peace.

Imagine someone is tapping you. You are trying to concentrate, but they're just tapping you with that solitary index finger. Tap tap tap tap tap. How annoying is it that? Furthermore, how distracting is that? It's tough to concentrate and complete the task with that person tapping you. Preparing for and giving birth is kind of like that. You don't want to be in the position of having to keep paying attention to what you're doing and to the commands given to you by your birth team. So, find out whatever is taking your peace.

Self-care is essential. Peace of mind is a necessity. Self-care is unattainable without having peace. Peace is not something that you have to pursue, and it's not something that others can give you. They may be able to guide you along the way, but they can't give it to you. You have to know that going in. Self-care and peace go hand-in-hand. And you are the person tasked with ensuring you have it. It must come from inside and be maintained from within.

You cannot have peace if you're not doing self-care. They both drive. They're both necessary because they work together in the machine that is you in your life. I know for me; I have to have 8 hours of sleep. I did not come to understand how important that was for my overall health, my mental health, my physical health my patience with my children. I did not know how much that would matter until I started getting more sleep. Now, as a new parent, that is going to be nearly impossible, and that's part of being a parent, especially young parents. I would suggest start identifying healthy selfishness now. Healthy in the sense that you are leaving room for you to be a priority as well. Saying to yourself, I will wash clothes tomorrow I am going to DVR my show and watch it tonight. Feeling selfish is something that parents struggle with overall. Taking that time now ensures this becomes a healthy habit as you go through parenthood. If you still think that it's selfish for you to want to have some time to yourself, let's kind of analyze that. Are there other issues at play as your child is hungry, but you're saying forget that I'm going to bed? No, of course not. Let's keep that in mind when you're trying to put that "selfish" label on yourself. Self-care is a buzzword that everyone is speaking to on some level, and there's a reason for that. It's because we are beginning to understand that we have to be our best for other people.

There is a saying that says that you can't pour out if you're not pouring into yourself, and we use that a lot in my help. I use it in my speeches; it helps the person hearing it to kind of understand that you are worth it. Being about yourself is not necessarily selfish, so your homework, as of this chapter, is to learn about self-care. Identify a regimen that would work for you. I spoke earlier about me needing sleep. I also know that crossword puzzles help me. It helps me work through my anxiety, and it gives me something to do while it challenges me. You want to start putting your regiment in place now. And know that you may have to tweak it after the child is born, especially if you don't have a lot of support around you. We will talk more about the support later. But every chapter I want to talk about having support. I don't want you to feel bad if you don't feel like you have support. But we have to get things in place so that we can make up for the absence of support. That may even mean you are making a plan and sticking to it. You may also have to be your own accountability partner. Holding your self-accountable to stick to the plan that you identify so that you can be the best mother or father that you can be. Here is your suggested self-care regimen while you're pregnant, but please feel free to come up with your own;

- Rest. Rest. Rest. You have to rest, especially during the second trimester you typically give this burst of energy. You still need to rest. Your body is working on caring for nurturing and protecting your child while still operating in his regular passion that uses a lot of energy. Have to be smart and then you have to stock up some rest because the first days after the hospital the first weeks are going to tap you out

- Find a hobby that is consistent with your life. I'd start with free and easily accessible. This ensures there are little barriers to you enjoying something you enjoy. For me, that was crossword puzzles in the newspaper. It was reading books for you; it could be drawing it could be knitting. It could be anything but try to find something that again is cheap, easily accessible, and satisfying. Free is better, but if you feel like you can afford to do that and get a hobby that costs a little money, that's okay. And when I say a little money, I mean in terms of our subscription.

- Save your money. How is this self-care, you ask? This is self-care because there's nothing more devastating than needing your child and feeling like you can't meet that need. Learn more about money- how to make it, how to budget it, and how to save it.

- Be mindful of your time. I have learned that being polite may not always be the best thing. If someone is taking your energy or they are putting you in a negative headspace, there is absolutely nothing wrong with excusing yourself from their presence. You also have to be planful with your time. Yes, it may be fun to go out kicking it today, but if you don't have time tomorrow to rest and you have a busy evening then Sunday, you don't have time to relax and have an active Sunday before you know it; it is the beginning of the workweek, and you have not had any time for you and, more importantly, time for your baby. You are at your best for your baby when you are at your best. So be mindful of your time.

- Check in your city for free supports and recreational activities. If you check Google, just be specific regarding when doing the

different types of Google searches. You may be surprised by
what you find. For instance, in Columbus, Ohio, some places
give out car seats when you attend the class. Some areas will
give out diapers or sites that will give out gift cards to new
moms, so if you're in town or call around and see what you can
do even though you're a young parent. Even if you may feel
like I don't. You are a mom. You do have what it takes. You do
know what to do. But just like anything else, you will need
practice, and that's okay get that practice by starting
somewhere the Bible talks about not despise Small
Beginnings. The reason we should not despise Small
Beginnings is that every step you take is building a foundation,
and once you gain that skill-set, you won't have to learn it
again. So, once you get good at identifying resources within
your community, you will always know how to look for help,
and when you need help. That is essential, that is
irreplaceable; that is the scale for you to have.

- Every aspect of myself that began to surface was another
opportunity for me to love and cultivate that part of me. With
you, it will be no different. You will always have the
responsibility to nurture and love on yourself. You cannot take
care of your child to the best of your ability if you are not
taken care of. Granted, there are limits to this. Get yourself
some tickets to a concert for you vs. paying the rent for you
and your child? No, that's not self-care; that's selfish. But
taking time to yourself to develop yourself? Yes! It's not only
essential; It is okay! We need that. As mothers, we tend to put
everyone and everything else before ourselves. But you don't
get a prize for being overworked and running on little sleep!
You just wear down quicker.

Here's your homework for this chapter:

- Identify things that make you happy! Happiness is subjective
as it is defined by you! Happiness can be the joy you get doing
a crossword puzzle, reading a book or watching a TV show

uninterrupted. Is it shopping? Talking on the phone? Meeting a friend for coffee?

- Can anyone help you?
- Who are you? What do you like? Equally important is what don't you like? Truly identify these things as they will be a platform for you as you continually walk this out.
- Identify the things you like about yourself and the things you want to change? Set goals for how to achieve these goals. You made need counseling or assistance for this, and that is okay!
- Take your "me time!" Don't unlearn this mindset. My children are now 21, 20, and 2, and I still need "me time." It makes me a better mom. Why? I am my own person. I am allowed to have some individuality concerning what I want, what I want to do, and how I relax. Yes, as mothers, our priorities shift to putting our families first. Rightfully so. Yet we cannot pour into our children or anyone else for that matter if we are not making sure we are cared for. Leave your child crying forever to watch Love and Hip Hop? No. But taking a bath, reading a book, taking a walk. Yes! There is a common-sense activity that you could do, even if it's sitting on the couch while the baby sleeps.
- Lastly, sleep while your baby sleeps!!!!! I cannot stress that enough, especially for new parents! The clothes will wash themselves. The cleaning will happen. But you need to be alert and attentive to your child, and without rest, how good can you be for them?

5

PARENTS JUST (DON'T) UNDERSTAND

As I wrote this, I smiled. Depending on the day, your parents can be your best friend and ally or an unexpected enemy. This is especially true if you have some other things going on. I wholeheartedly believe this, both as a parent and a child. During my childhood, my mother and I were close. Despite the difficulties in the home due to my parents' issues. I was relied on heavily, and I looked forward to being there for my family. At times she relied on me, seemingly putting me in the place of a peer. Although I didn't see it, then I can see now that I was a parentified child. I also see now my father made me responsible for my younger siblings as well as carrying adult burdens. At that moment, I sincerely felt I did all that was asked of me. All that I felt was required of me and experienced all that I have experienced without being unaffected by the things I experienced, saw, and heard. As a social worker, I am quite sure that it is not accurate. I now know that I was being traumatized. As much as I love my parents, I have to acknowledge how they were selfish at times. Putting their needs and desires above my need to grow into a healthy adult. As I further evaluate my childhood as a parent, now further enables my ability to acknowledge this as a fact.

By the time I was pregnant, my mother was in a relationship with a weak man who fueled her strong crack habit. My mother was a broken person. Early on in my life, I often pitied her, excusing the abuse she would mete out because I loved her. If she had ever learned this, she would have been furious with me. Pity is not something she ever wanted from anyone. Her life was crazy, and the abuse she endured far outweighed mine and was worthy of compassion, but she would not hear of it. Nevertheless, in my mind, I thought that excusing people's behavior and standing with them regardless of that behavior is what you do when you love someone. I sincerely thought this is what unconditional love looks like: taking everything they throw at you and never walking away or hurting them back. That mindset would come back to haunt me several times in my life, but it was initially challenged with my first child.

My son and I were sitting at the table, and I was preparing to feed him breakfast when I heard my mother stir behind me. She had been napping on the couch. It was morning, and just the three of us in the home as my siblings had gone on to school. William's eyes shifted to his grandmother, who was making her way toward her grandbaby. I smiled, putting the spoon back in the oatmeal, knowing there was no way he would continue eating now. I glanced at the melting butter pooling on the oatmeal and figured we had time. I sat back and watched my son now reaching for her with happy anticipation.

"Good morning, my baby," she sang. Her nightgown ebbed and flowed around her small frame, seemingly making room for him to sit on her hip. He cooed and flailed his chunky chocolate legs.

"Deanna, what are you feeding him"? She asked bewildered. My son snuggled into her, now no longer hungry.

"Oatmeal," I stated flatly, confused by her confusion. We looked at each other briefly, trying to understand where the other's head was.

"No wonder he's not eating that." She turned to Elias stating, "I'm going to fix you a good breakfast" and started toward the kitchen with my son. Instantly I was incensed. My eyes stung with tears of frustration. I grew angrier as I sat and stewed, my body growing more rigid with restraint. I knew that having an opinion was not often allowed when it contracted hers, but this day, I am going to have one and take whatever is thrown at me

"Um, mom, this is fine. You can cook him something if you like, but he is eating this". I moved in to take him from my mother and sat him back in his chair. My body grew tense, not knowing what to expect.

"He's not going to eat that. It looks like slop, and it's cold". I looked down at the bowl, and sure enough, it had cooled. The butter had congealed and bonded the oats together, leaving nothing but a uniformed layer of oats. My eyes rolled for a good 10 seconds in my head. *Dang, why did this have to be cold?! It looks like I can spackle a wall!* I thought.

"Mom, it was- "but she cut me off.

"Deanna, I am going to cook him some real food. I don't know why you are feeding him that mess."

"Because he likes it!" I exclaim.

"Does he"? she challenged as she continued to cook. Right then, I had to decide how far I was going to take this conversation. With my mom, this could easily be blown out of proportion. I shook my head in resignation and resumed feeding my son. I did not want to fight. I didn't want the conflict, but she did.

"He's not going to eat it," she called out from the kitchen. She began to mumble about me, my decisions as a parent, and me as a person. She came into the dining room and sat at the table behind William. She attempted to turn my son toward her, but I was holding the seat with my legs.

"Mom, I am not done. "

"Yes, you are. He doesn't like that".

"Mom, you don't like this for him, but he likes it. Watch." As if on cue, my son decided to stop eating the oatmeal. She took this as all of the confirmation she needed.

"See told you," she says, now scolding me angrily for "disrespecting her" by offering a dissenting opinion. My eyes began to sting with tears. Fighting their way out of my eyes while holding it together.

"I didn't disrespect you..." I started. As much as I tried, I wasn't able to keep it together. "I decide what he eats. I decide when he eats. I am fine with him eating what you have fixed, but me stating he needs to finish eating this oatmeal first is not disrespectful". At this point, I attempt to leave the room, knowing that this convo was getting ready to go off of the deep end. I stand on the carpet and begin to take the bowl into the kitchen.

"Listen, bitch. I am trying to help you. All of a sudden, I don't know shit? Like I ain't been a mother to yo' ass all this time." She continues to cuss, and rail about her perceived slights. I continue to stand in the kitchen, listening. I don't want my son to see my crying. I don't want him to see an argument, but today it's not looking good.

I return to the dining room and begin to take my son out of his high chair.

"Now what"? She asked incredulously. "Oh, you mad," she asks.

"Mom, I don't want you talking like that in front of him. Especially over oatmeal. I already said he could eat what you fixed. You are not going to disrespect me in front of my son. I am not taking that". I could feel the tension rising from her, and I braced myself for what was to come next. Not sure if I was going to be hit or worse, but I was prepared to take it. My eyes were transfixed on her, but my focus was around our home. I looked at the wood paneling on the walls. My eyes traveled slowly across the paneling as it bowed and swayed at will on the wall. The silence was brief but seemed to last forever, allowing me to continue my scan of the dining room. While waiting for what was to come, I noticed the dingy carpet and the stains that made their own pattern on the floor, waiting for what was to come. She threw the spoon onto the table and said, "Fine. Do what you want". The rest of the day, she was short with me. The next day or two, it slowed, but I couldn't get much help from her, and then you know what happened? She was over it. She loved her grandchild, and she loved me. She sincerely wanted to help. It was a lesson that we both needed to learn. Her role as my mother was NOT an automatic carryover or override key in her role as a grandmother. I can say now it was worth it, but 16-year-old Deanna was not so sure. I had begun the journey to setting and enforcing boundaries and advocating for what is best for my child.

As a mother, I care very much about what is best for my child, as most parents do. Even as a young parent, this was true, and it is certainly true today. I have little tolerance for things or people that hurt my babies. Especially since I made so much effort to protect them from as much as I can! That desire fueled so many of my life choices, personally and professionally. As a career, I chose to enter into the social work field to be an advocate for those who can't speak for themselves. Whether by a limitation such as age and size or never having learned. This desire to advocate was on display early and often in my life. It was even stronger as a parent, so when these two roles in my life, advocate, and devoted daughter, butted heads, I had a decision to make. I was at a strategic inflection point. I did not like disappointing my parents in any way. I also did not like it when anyone attempted to override my decisions related to what I decided was the best choice for my child. I didn't care if I was impolite, or your feelings got hurt. Subsequently, when my mother and I were at an impasse, I didn't care that she was MY mother.

I only cared that I was HIS mother. He is my son, and the final say was mine. Period. The irony for the conflict was lost on my mother. This is exactly who she was as a parent. It didn't matter if it was her mother or my father; what she said was what it was. That's what I saw moms do. Logically, that made sense to me. Protective parents said what needed to be said and did what needed to be done to ensure that my child's needs were met and that he was living his best life. The juxtaposition between my role and a mother and a role as a daughter continued to give rise to conflict and more abuse, but I endured it. It was an up and down ride with my parents. We often danced, trying to find the rhythm for this new dynamic, trying to see who would lead. Time would soon bear out that it was my mother and me that were in the dance, learning new moves along the way.

. . .

My mother was hands-on and insisted that I do things her way. As my mother and I danced, my father never stepped onto the floor. In his mind, it was my responsibility, and that was it. He was genuinely hands-off most of the time. This was very evident when I had my children. The way they operated as parents would bear out in their roles as grandparents and as a support for me in my new role; mother. My mother would yell at me when I would be holding my children wrong or attempt to direct me in what I should feed my son. Even to this day, when I discipline my now-adult son, she cautions me not to be too hard on him.

Even today, she reminded me how I would bring him to her when I need to get some sleep and INSTANTLY (in her mind at least) he would go to sleep. Or like the time mentioned above when she didn't like how I made his instant oatmeal and got up instead to fix this 11-month-old some pancakes and scrambled eggs, excuse me? I marvel at the mindset she had. She, too, felt as if she wanted to ensure he had the best but didn't consider that it was not her role to provide that *best*. Parents do have some adjustments to make, just like you do. Parents at this stage are probably really inconsistent. Some days they are very supportive, seeing eye to eye with you, and other days you will not understand how they can think the way that they do.

Don't forget that your parents are also in a new place. They are still your parents. Here they are looking at their daughter, who is not yet grown, responsible for another human being. As a parent, let me tell you, they are scared. Some parents take a more hands-on approach and try to do everything with you and for you, while others are the exact opposite and allow you to do most of the leg work. This is a spectrum, and there are varying points in between. Please remember that they are still responsible to parent and guide you. There will be times when this clashes with YOUR role as a parent.

As a teenager or young adult, your parents still have their parental instinct in full overdrive. It will, indeed, take time to adjust. You have to prepare for that. This way, you can be patient and mindful of your interactions with them. As a parent, you have the absolute right to have the last say when it comes to your children. No one can or should try to take that from you. I do think that does need to be tempered or weighed against the wisdom that your parents may be able to offer you! As in most things in life, experience is the best teacher, and your parents have a wealth of it. Granted, no one's parents are perfect. Not me and not your parents, however, knowing that you are new to this be open to their suggestions. They can suggest things that will make your life so much more comfortable both by knowing what works and what does not. If you can avoid their pitfalls by listening to them, why wouldn't you? You and your child will both be better off for it. It's the simple things parents can add that will make your life so much easier.

For me, it was how to sterilize and prepare the bottles ahead of time and have them in the fridge. Napping when your baby is napping. I would have realized this knowledge eventually, but I do think that having it before I needed it was a godsend.

Now, I would be remiss if I did not acknowledge that there are some parents who, unfortunately, cannot be the asset, and ally, they should be for you. Please know that you are still going to be successful. It may be harder to go about things, but in all honesty, it may not be. I have the unique perspective of having my parents as a teen parent and then not having them. Yes, as a teen parent. For me, drugs and alcohol caused my father and mother's relationship to swing between two extremes. After a touch and go presence with my mom staying in a trap house and staying in the home, she eventually went back to prison. My father treated me as an adult and subsequently left me home to raise my children and my younger siblings. Granted, they were one and two years younger than me, respectively, but that I should not have to raise them along with my two babies at 16 and ½, but I did. This was my reality as a new parent. No schooling, no support, but as a parent. I came through that, and you can come through too.

I had no thought or concern regarding our new roles. As a teenager, I felt like it was pretty self-explanatory. In reality, not so much. As an adult, I would try to balance the dual roles that my parents and I would share. Thinking of your baby now, I must ask. If you saw your child doing something wrong, would you help them? What if they refused? They what? It's hard to say so imagine when you're in the situation, and you don't have that time to process this? You do the best that you can in that moment. You are the parent, but know that you are still a child. You are not automatically "grown "because you are pregnant.

Here are some final reminders as we close this chapter;

- Be gracious! You have the right to say no, but be mindful you are talking to your parents!
- Remember, this is your child. With great power comes great responsibility. The decisions that affect your child belong to you, his mom/dad. With that comes the outcome of that decision. Be mindful of that. Evaluate when to say no. Just because you CAN say, no doesn't mean that you should. Do what you feel is best for your child, regardless of whose idea it was.
- Know that it's okay to change your mind. If you decide to do something your way but you see it is not working, it's okay to say, "mom, dad, I think you were right. Can you help me"?
- Your parents are an asset to you! They are your ally. They will have your back and, subsequently, the back of your child. Do not be afraid to get them on board with you what you have planned for you and your child's' future.
- If you do not have parental support, can you find adult support or a permanent connection for you? Just let it happen naturally. In the meantime, focus on doing the best that you can with the resources available. Books, like this one, are a wealth of information. Use all that you can. Also, look and see if you can find a support group or some group you can fellowship with. Any support is better than not. And you will need it no matter how strong you are!
- Take the help! Your parents more than likely have been where you are. If they raised you, they have something to share. They have a mindset they can teach.

✾ 6 ✾

WHAT DOES POSTPARTUM DEPRESSION HAVE TO DO WITH ME?

Mothers are notorious for putting the needs of the family first. That is both a blessing and a curse. I feel that this will never go away. My kids that I had as a teenager are 22 and 23 as of this book. I decided to have My baby is 4 (yes, I know...what was I thinking). I still put them first. When they were younger, that was all I did. They were dressed in the most beautiful clothing. They had several choices in the average day to day wear, all of which were nice while I dressed like a pauper. I thought that was one of the attributes of a good mother. I did not want to be the type of woman who had her hair done, and her child's' hair was not or had on nice clothing, but my child did not. That, coupled with preparation in every area of their lives, was equal to anything I had going. Granted, I still think like that, but I have learned balance! As a new mom, it is easy to give your all. Being depleted and neglecting self-care does not make you a "good mom." PLEASE DON'T DO THIS.

As a new mother, I encourage you to be mindful of your time and your peace. Count it as precious! I have learned that being polite may not always be the best thing. If someone is taking your energy or they are putting you in a negative headspace, there is absolutely nothing wrong with excusing yourself from their presence. You also have to be planful with your time. Yes, it may be fun to go out kicking it today, but if you don't have time tomorrow to rest and you have a busy evening then Sunday, you don't have time to rest and have an active Sunday before you know it; it is the beginning of the workweek, and you have not had any time for you and, more importantly, time for your baby. You are at your best for your baby when you are at your best. So be mindful of your time.

I genuinely believe not treating your self-care and, subsequently, your peace as precious may heighten the likelihood of developing postpartum depression. When one hears this phrase, it may invoke the image of an inept parent, overwhelmed, crying, or despondent. Yes, both of those may be how you experience postpartum depression. It is important to note this is not the only way it is manifested. Knowing other symptoms will assist you and your doctor, ensuring it is not missed and can address it if you start seeing these symptoms.

On that note, Postpartum depression is just that, a form of *DEPRESSION*. I have struggled with depression and anxiety since I was 17 years old, and let me say this is very much a REAL issue. It is common, so please understand most women experience this but to varying degrees. A simple Google search can speak to the vastness of PPD. I have found one that I think could be very helpful. This list provides other signs of postpartum that may be overlooked. According to Postpartumprogress.com, here are some things to watch out for.

Postpartum Depression Symptoms

Okay. Here we go. You may have **postpartum depression** if you have had a baby within the last 12 months and are experiencing *some* of these symptoms:

- You feel overwhelmed. Not like "hey, this new mom thing is hard." More like, "I can't do this, and I'm never going to be able to do this." You feel like you just can't handle being a mother. You may be wondering whether you should have become a mother in the first place.
- You feel guilty because you believe you should be handling new motherhood better than this. You feel like your baby

deserves better. You worry whether your baby can tell that you feel so bad, or that you are crying so much, or that you don't feel the happiness or connection that you thought you would. You may wonder whether your baby would be better off without you.

- You don't feel bonded to your baby. You're not having that mythical mommy bliss that you see on TV or read about in magazines. Not everyone with postpartum depression feels this way, but many do.

- You can't understand why this is happening. You are very confused and scared.

- You feel irritated or angry. You have no patience. Everything annoys you. You feel resentment toward your baby, or your partner, or your friends who don't have babies. You feel out-of-control rage.

- You feel nothing. Emptiness and numbness. You are just going through the motions.

- You feel sadness in the depths of your soul. You can't stop crying, even when there's no real reason to be crying.

- You feel hopeless like this situation will never get better. You feel weak and defective, like a failure.

- You can't bring yourself to eat, or perhaps the only thing that makes you feel better is eating.

- You can't sleep when the baby sleeps, nor can you sleep at any other time. Or maybe you can fall asleep, but you wake up in the middle of the night and can't go back to sleep no matter how tired you are. Or maybe all you can do is sleep, and you can't seem to stay awake to get the most basic things done. Whichever it is, your sleeping is completely screwed up, and it's not just because you have a newborn.

- You can't concentrate. You can't focus. You can't think of the words you want to say. You can't remember what you were supposed to do. You can't make a decision. You feel like you're in a fog.

- You feel disconnected. You feel strangely apart from everyone like there's an invisible wall between you and the rest of the world.

- Maybe you're doing everything right. You are exercising. You are taking your vitamins. You have a healthy spirituality. You do yoga. You're thinking, "Why can't I just get over this?" You feel like you should be able to snap out of it, but you can't.
- You might be having thoughts of running away and leaving your family behind. Or you've thought of driving off the road, taking too many pills, or finding some other way to end this misery.
- You know something is wrong. You may not know you have a perinatal mood or anxiety disorder, but you know the way you are feeling is NOT right. You think you've "gone crazy."
- You are afraid that this is your new reality and that you've lost the "old you" forever.
- You are afraid that if you reach out for help, people will judge you. Or that your baby will be taken away. (www. postpartumprogress.com/the-symptoms-of-postpartum-depression-anxiety-in-plain-english)

If you are feeling any of these symptoms, please take care of yourself by getting the help that you need. The easiest way to "take care of yourself" is to pay attention to you! Take note of how often you are feeling what you are feeling. If you find yourself increasingly sad, feeling your life is over, discouraged, and without hope, please take the opportunity to speak to someone about these feelings. If you can, write down when you are feeling any of the things in this chapter. It may help you to track and provide a clearer picture to decide if you are experiencing this and the best course of action to address it. It can sneak up on you! After my last son, I found myself increasingly forgetful. I can remember one instance in particular.

I was on my way to see my counselor. I knew that it was time; something was off, but I was not sure. I had looked around to find a counselor able to counsel me. Being a foster child and a caseworker, I knew there were levels to this. A degree tells me you completed the work, but it doesn't tell me your method of application in helping me.

It doesn't tell me your rationale and your ability to be objective or comforting, but I'll digress. I only lived about 5 minutes away, but 22 minutes later, I found myself jarred back to reality. I was at a stop sign waiting for it to change. My windows were down, and my music was blaring as usual. I grew impatient waiting for them to change, but I found myself content with the forced pause. I watched the winds play tag with the leaves. A little further down the street, some kids were running around their yard, oblivious to the world around them. I glanced up and looked to see if the stop sign had changed to green. *No change,* I thought. *That's odd.* I continued to wait. The warm breezes found their way into my car and began to carry away my cares. I began singing aloud, and before you knew it, I had decided that I was going to keep looking at this sign until it changes to green. So, I did. *Why won't this change to green?!* I wondered aloud. Again, I grew impatient until the horn behind me sounded. I honked the horn back and yelled in defiance, "What am I supposed to do, you see the light"!

The pair in the car behind me looked at each other then at me. A passerby yelled across the street.

"What are you doing?" He asked as he continued to his destination.

"What"? I asked. He didn't reply but pointed at the sign. The stop sign. It was not a light and, therefore, would never change. Embarrassed, I put up a hand in apologies and began to pull forward. I could not wait to tell my counselor about this.

In her office, I relayed the events just before my arrival. She listened and asked me if I had any other instances like this. I had! I had been driving and have no memory of arriving at my destination. I have forgotten simply things, and my memory continued to grow worse by the day. She explained to me postpartum depression and how it manifests in various ways. I had some other contributing factors, but indeed I was diagnosed with it. I initially denied this, feeling that I had not felt any sadder. We completed an assessment, and then she showed me the results. There, in black and white, was overwhelming proof. We began to address it, and instantly I felt lighter. Was I all better? No, but it felt good to have a plan and some understanding about what I am experiencing.

In sharing this, I am hoping you see that I, too, experienced a manifestation a little different than the normal. Take advantage of your supports where you can! Don't let proximity or cost keep you from caring for you. There are support groups that are free or on a sliding scale. Reach out to them. You may also ask your primary care doctor for directives. They may help point you in the right direction. Lastly, your insurance may have a program that can provide you with assistance. You have to start by asking. Please do not dismiss it, downplay it, or think that you can just power through. Even if you are successful at first, that will not last. You are not weak or a bad mom. On the contrary, you are demonstrating that you are quite the opposite. I do not like the idea of "Good mom/Bad mom," but I am using the terminology I hear mom's use. Please try and not evaluate yourself using good and bad, nor by comparing your mothering style to another!

It takes a strong person to admit that he or she is weak. It requires more of you! You have to be vulnerable enough to admit it. You have to honest when it's not easy to admit it. And you have to accept the help. In covering up and trying to plow through, you aren't viewed as vulnerable or anything like that.

- Be proactive regarding your self-care! If you begin to notice any of the above, just watch how you are feeling and what works to alleviate those feelings. Maintain your care as you care for your child. You cannot care for your child's needs if yours are not met within reason.
- Learn all you can about Postpartum disorder. If you know the warning signs, you can seek help.
- Seek help early! If you know that you see signs of something simply, "not right," then seek help. Google searches are key to generation, and it can help here too! Use it to your advantage.
- Do you have a friend or family member that can be a partner in addressing and overcoming your PPD? Accountability

coaches are great. They don't have to be professionals. Set out some signs that if they see they can pull you aside and discuss it, that continues to be an issue for you. If you have that person, turn to a professional.

- Lastly, have your own rubric, so to speak, to determine when you need to seek help. Look at the signs. Seek out some other resources to ensure you have as good of an understanding as you can have. So, when you establish your own self-assessment, you can be as accurate as possible.

NOPE. IT'S STILL NOT LIKE TV;
THE CULTURE OF PARENTHOOD

I remember looking at motherhood on TV as a young mother. It very easily misrepresents what it means to be a mother. Look at the mothers that I saw on TV growing up. I saw the beautiful and Infamous Clair Huxtable from The Cosby Show. Although she is a fictional character, she is the epitome of a great mother. She was classy, professional, smart, and was always there for her husband and her children. Who in the world can compete with that?? I knew that I couldn't, but it was my goal. Another mother I grew up with was Peg Bundy from *Married with Children*. Now I'm definitely showing my age with these references but bear with me. Peg was a self-absorbed stay at home mom who was the bon-bon eating, couch surfing, daytime TV show watching Queen. Her children lived their lives; however, they wanted to. She stayed spending money and dressed up. She still lived her life; however, she wanted, never cooked or cleaned, or even bought food.

Among the other TV shows, we see a variety of mothers. Some portrayed mothers who were utterly devoted and coming in from work immediately cooking doing everything that they can. In contrast, others put themselves last to make sure everyone else was alright. What strikes me now is they rarely show these moms, even Peg Bundy, being frustrated, being sad, or being overwhelmed. As a young mother looked at these mothers and real-life mothers wondering how does any mom get anything done? How in the world do we do it all? Well, the reality of it is we don't do it all. We are human and have limitations. What does ALL look like to you? More than likely, the ALL you use to determine your success as a mother is based on your culture.

In my opinion, how you interpret motherhood will depend heavily on the culture in which you were or are currently being raised. For me, motherhood was something that all women would want to do. It was a different type of love, selfless, and very painful at times but worth it. With that, the culture of your home, family, neighborhood, gender, race, etc. all play a role in how you view the world, including the world of motherhood.

Culture has a variety of different avenues and caveats to its meaning. In essence, it is everything that makes you who you are! Think about how many aspects of you there are. The best way to imagine culture is to picture a glacier. Now I know right now you're thinking I *KNOW* she is not about to talk to me about a Glacier or about culture. Again, I ask for you to bear with me. Yes, I am! There is a method to my madness.

You see the ice and snow at the top of the glacier (Figure 1). In short, it is a floating mountain of ice. It is a mountain, and it is enormous (Figure 2)! If asked to assess this glacier, you have to consider everything you see. But what about what you don't see? Now let's look at the entire glacier.

Figure 1

Figure 2

Here we see how much of the glacier lies underneath! Underneath your exterior (or what people see), what is there that makes you who you are? Underneath are those experiences (good and bad) values, religion, comfort, things you do for fun, what is normal, what is acceptable, etc. Those will form your perception of the world, including motherhood! With that, let's look at these pictures of my life.

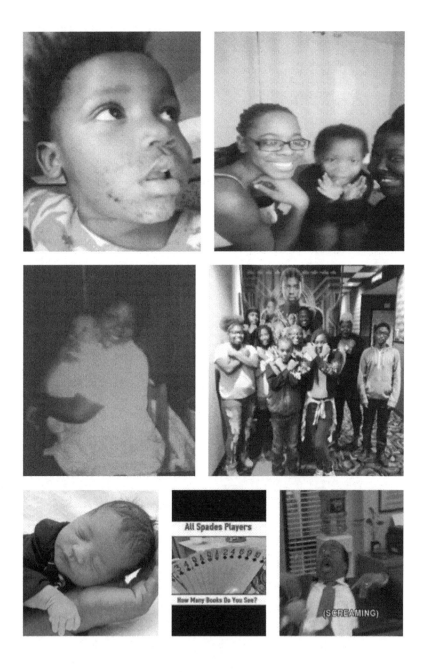

What do you feel they tell you about me? How would you describe my culture? Motherhood in and of itself is open to "interpretation." You hear what makes a *good* or a *real* mother, a *black* vs. a *white* mother, but all of that is up to interpretation. Granted, generally, some experiences and values are found in each culture, and the culture of motherhood is no different. These values may be applied, more or less, across the board. Still, a lot of those experiences and values will depend on your interpretation. So, why are we talking about motherhood and culture?? There will be times where the two clash and intersect. Motherhood will intersect with who you are underneath at various aspects of your beliefs, practices, etc. Your culture. Historically, my culture allowed mothers to feed their babies what they wanted when they wanted, and the mother still held to this. I did not agree with that at all. I avoided processed foods, excess sugar (if at all), and aimed for organic foods. My mother took upon herself to feed my child what she deemed okay as if she could override my wishes for my child. And she was serious, you guys. She was in utter disbelief that I checked. Softly, yes, but I did check her. I had to remind her of her role; and the permissions (note the word used there) that came with it. She felt that as the grandmother, she could feed my mother anything she wants, including frozen pot pies and sips of sprite, even at 11 months! That's what motherhood meant to her, but not to me! To her, "a little bit won't hurt." To me, that is harmful in so many ways. I genuinely believe that the way you lived as a kid may have things you could do better, and if you identify them, then you owe it to your child to do that. I stand on that even unto this day.

In the culture of my childhood home, what your mom says is the law, and to challenge that is disrespectful. Yes, even as an adult, my mother felt this way. Luckily, my mother grew to know my dissenting as a daughter, not being disrespectful, all the more so as an adult. In my role as a mother, I don't care who you are! MY word is the law. Given the duality of the mother and daughter roles, there was definitely room for conflict. All of the interactions are not going to be bad or have a negative spin. As a mother to her grandchild and as my mother, she would cook for us both and spoil us in little ways (once she began to come around). To this day, my mom will come over and cook for me if I am sick, will watch my 4-year-old so I can nap or ensure he has the little things. I am glad to see how far we've come. Just know that at the intersection of mother and daughter, expect that time where your roles may present a challenge and prepare accordingly. It may help to have that conversation early and often. I encourage you to be as honest as you can, and above all else, be respectful!

As we close out this chapter regarding the culture of parenthood I want to leave you with this; don't fall for the comparison trap. As parents, we often find ourselves evaluating our success with our children. It makes sense! We want to do the best we can to ensure our children are able to do and have whatever they want. We want to see them excel in every way we didn't and every way we did! It is also nice to simply see the sacrifices and the effort were not in vain! On that journey to make sure our children have their best foot forward in this life is where you could fall for that trap; comparing yourself to the next parent. Don't. Please don't. There is an old adage that says, *comparison is the thief of joy.* In all that time you are comparing yourself you are missing the joys that parenthood affords you! Comparison also steals the experience on the journey. Some lessons you can learn from watching others, undoubtedly. Other things benefit you far more if you can experience them for yourself.

I truly believe parents are trying to do the best that they can with the resources available to them. Most parents put their children first and make decisions with their children's best interest in mind. Allow yourself space to learn from your mistakes and experiences. There is nothing wrong with gaining advice from other mothers but when you feel your success/failure is tied up in matching the next parent you have lost. When you consider the definition of motherhood make sure you temper it with a livable definition of motherhood. . Don't make the standard unrealistically unattainable. You don't need the added stress, trust me. Please know though, you're going to mess up. Even for your own things you're going to miss the mark. As a new mom let me simply say to you learn how to forgive yourself for early and often. Great you need to learn from your mistakes but don't dwell in them. That does not help you and it does not help your child.

- Here I would start (or continue) to frame what motherhood means to you and to make sure that it is realistic.
- What are your goals for yourself as a mother? What are your goals for your children? What are any barriers to these goals and what could you put in place to address it? What do you hope to accomplish today? By the end of the week? What are your long-term goals for you and your children? Setting goals will help you see what you have accomplished and give you a clear picture of not only what Is needed but what goals to set next!
- Identify any ideas or thoughts that are unrealistic or unhealthy regarding being a parent. Yes, even the culture you identify with, familiarly, racially, or any other means to identify culturally.
- Practice forgiving yourself now! You are going to do something you may deem "wrong". We are humans who happen to be parents and still make mistakes. You have to be able to forgive yourself. You will have to forgive yourself to go on being a parent and to learn from your mistakes.

❧ 8 ❧

MY CHILD'S FATHER (MOTHER) IS
_____?

Reflect on this question. What is the role your child's other parent will play in the life of you and your child's lives? What do you want the interaction between you and that other parent to reflect? Any answer to these questions or any other will more than likely yield a different answer depending on where you are in your life. As a teenager I would have said simply that my children's father was "Corey". I expect him to provide for half of everything they need. We would have to have an open relationship to communicate for our kids. If you ask me today about Corey, I would say he chose to stay out of my children's lives. I very rarely speak negatively of him, even to this day. I encourage you to follow suit when it comes to the other person in their lives. I wanted my children to have the freedom, true freedom, to reach their OWN unbiased opinion of their father. It doesn't benefit you or your children. Don't speak badly about the absent parent. Ladies, that includes your face and body language! Men that will include your actions! It doesn't really matter why the parent is not present, it matters most that you have to do it on your own for a while.

I could have easily spoken badly about my kids' father. He had admitted to me that he got me pregnant on purpose. I am not sure what the rationale was but it changed my life forever. If you will recall, earlier in this book I touched on the fact that I didn't want children. I had a plan for my life and it was all about me. I was going to work, get out of my neighborhood and move on to do all of these *great things*. Yet, years later my kids father admittedly impregnated me on purpose he then decided to leave when his whole plan didn't come to fruition. There I was...14 and pregnant. I didn't know what else to do? I knew I wasn't going to have an abortion and so I had my son. He drifted away and I was determined that I would not beg him to stay. I reached out to him every so often but the time between my efforts to reach out grew more and more until they stopped. Finally, one day we showed up on my door step.

I remember this day so clearly. I was in my kitchen cooking; my children playing in their room when I heard a knock at the door. Something about this knock was so familiar. I walked the short distance from the stove to the front door. I marveled as I swung open the door. There he stood, still slightly taller than me. It was eerie how my son resembled him. I stared at him blankly. I couldn't believe it yet there he stood in the stark yellow hallway light. He put his hands in my pockets and leaned his head to the side with wide eyes. *Geez,* I thought, *those are by baby's eye lashes.*

"Can I come in"? He finally asked. I didn't respond but did step back and allow him into my apartment. It was my first apartment out of foster care so it left a lot to be desired. My eyes searched the apartment looking for another point of focus but found none so I refocused on him. Now it was his turn for his eyes to travel. His glaze drunk in my little apartment. The apartment was stark materially but filled with love. The walls were the color of vanilla ice cream. The floor was tan with brown streaks. Even when it was clean it looked dirty. It seemed the tiles were made of dirt. There was one couch in the front room and a lone TV. The paper blinds closed and opened allowing in the sounds of the neighborhood below. Listening to the police sirens and the drunken revelry on the porch below helped to bring me back. He walked over toward the TV stand that held not only out tv but our books as well. I watched him as he turned to me.

"What do you want"? I asked him flatly. He nodded looking around, finding our wall of excellence. Any award my children earned I put on the wall behind us. It was covered from ceiling to the floor with awards in chronological order. Once it was full I those into a photo album and started all over again. I leave to finish flipping my chicken before returning to the front room. The whole apartment was about 700 square feet but it felt like there was a football field between us.

"I .... uh... wanted to say hi" he said. I could tell he was grasping at straws, trying to have a normal conversation but I wasn't there yet. I knew he was uneasy but I had no desire to set him at ease and continued to meet out my cool indifference

"Um...hi". I reply. I lean on the doorway of the doorframe between the kitchen and dining room.

He smiled and returned to the wall. "My kids did all of this"? He asked with a small smile on his face. Any vestige of restraint I had left as the words and all of the motion I thought I had a handle on broke free from my lips.

"No. MY kids". I state matter of factly. "They are my kids".

"Look- "He starts but I was not finished.

"No, you look. I am glad that you decided to come by and say hi but don't make that mistake again. These are my kids". Suddenly I began to shake. Tears of frustration filled my eyes and my old coping skill kicked in; resignation. I knew that I didn't want to be the reason he didn't see Tallia and William. I didn't want them to blame me. I tried to soften my approach. "Corey, I don't understand what you are doing here. You come by to say hi?!"

"Yes." He nodded. "I wasn't sure what else to say. I missed you. I missed them."

"You don't even know them". *Shoot, I have got to get better at this.* I thought.

"I know. I know" He exclaimed. Again, silence filled the room. Out the corner of my eye movement. We both shifted our attention to the two little bodies standing on the edge of the room. They stared at the stranger and the elephant in the room.

"Mommy. Who's this?" Tallia asks. She walks a little further in the room, William alongside. Before I could respond Corey answered.

"I am your dad". He says softly. He smiled and knelt down, slightly offering his arms out in the hopes of a hug. They hung there before he realized neither child had moved. He stood; his face slightly crushed. "Well. I tried". He says looking at me.

"Did you? Is that an attempt? They don't know you Corey. I am not going to stand in the way but you have to put in the work to establish your own relationship with them. Just know this. You not going to be running in and out of their lives." He nodded and this time I offered him a seat on the couch. I sat and picked up the kids.

"You guys this is your dad. Although he has not been around but he wanted to come now and get to know you. Mommy is okay with this. Are you okay with this? Is that okay?" I paused waiting for a response. William didn't respond. He looked at Corey and then laid on me. Tallia stared at Corey. She didn't say anything but wrapped my arm around her and nodded. I looked at Corey and sighed. *I wonder how long this will last* I wondered. Unfortunately, not long.

Soon after that the attempts at connecting with my kids became second fiddle to kicking it with my younger brother. Before long, I was asking Corey for help and he wasn't giving it. After a few times of asking for diapers or snack I again accepted provision was not something I can look for from them. I soon turned my attention to asking when he would see the kids. Worker offered to leave and let my cousin be here if the conflict between the two of proved too much for him. He declined and stated he wants to see me too. He promised things would get better but they never did. He continued setting and missing more and more appointments for ice cream or trips to the library. The last appointment came and went. This time, I decided it was the last time.

I decided while I put the children in the tub, I would grab the cordless and give him a call. The phone rang and my stomach began to sink. I knew this was not going to end well.

"Hey girl, what's up" He answered jovially. *Are you kidding me?!* I thought.

"Corey, I just called to see why you were playing my kids?"

"Playing them how"? He asked. I sat quietly, knowing he knows the answer. "Okay, is this about me not coming to pick them up?

"What else would it be about"? I asked watching the children play. *This dude is freaking crazy. I should just hang up. I can't with this* I thought. "Corey, I brought them to you. I told you I don't have to be there you can visit with my cousin present and that wasn't enough. What the hell are you doing?"

"And who told you do that" He countered.

"Do what?"

"Have your cousin there. You were supposed to be there".

"No, I don't have to be there. You are there to see them. Not me."

"Well, I still don't understand why you won't let me spend the night".

"You can. On the couch".

"No, you are baby's mom. I am supposed to be able to – "

"No. No! You are not entitled to anything. You either are going to take care of your kids or not".

"In that case. Not." He says coolly.

"Not? Not what? As in if I don't have sex with you then you don't want to take care of your kids?" Tears fill my eyes and I look down to see Tallia and William playing. I stand and turn. *I am tired of them seeing me cry.* "Man, I can't believe- "

"Listen, If I can't have you…If I can't have the whole thing, I don't want any of it".

"What"?

"You heard me. I don't think this is for me" He said dismissively.

"You got ME pregnant"! yelled. I began to pace in the small hallway just outside of the bathroom, pointing as if he could see me.

"I am young. I am not ready for this" He snapped.

"Ready? Ready for what? I was 15 when I gave birth. You were 18. What – "

"When I am ready, I will come and get them" he offered, "Goodbye". Just like that... he was gone. Just as quickly as he re-entered my life he left; once again leaving me a young, single parent.

I could have focused on that, allowed bitterness to enter in and set up a residence in my heart and even my soul! I could allow anger to permeate my being, and quite honestly for a moment it did, but in the end what would it change? Nothing. How will that aid me providing for my family? It didn't! So, I am grateful that I was able to focus not on his absence but being MORE to my children.

True, there are things that are intuitive to being a man that I cannot teach BUT I can most. definitely try! Get your haircut every week! Make sure your shoes are clean! Make sure your nails are clean, women notice that. A man's word IS his bond-keep your word son! I can teach him what women do like versus what they don't like. I can teach him how to be a provider. I can teach him to be a gentleman. I can teach him what God's word, society and what I understand what makes him a man. I can be sure that there are good and godly men around him that can be an example and a sounding board for things I could not discuss, due to his discomfort or my lack of knowledge. Let me say, I had to resolve that I have to be comfortable with everything and anything my son could say. Everyone's tolerance will not be the same to be able to discuss things to the same degree but be prepared to discuss!

In my later years I have a new child, Elias. He is so amazing. I would say that his father and I are determined to be the best co-parents for him. We are able to laugh, joke and communicate. We speak often about what is best for our son and the best way to do it. I am grateful for that. I took what I learned from Corey and built on it to have a great foundation for Elias' dad.

We have had to work through things to be to be at this point. We had to establish ground rules for respecting each other and each other's wishes. There are things that I don't worry about yet they are of up the upmost importance for Elias' father. For instance, I do not put a hat on Elias' head every time we leave the house when the temperature is 40 degrees and higher. His father feels like if Elias has on a coat or jacket Elias should have on a hat. Knowing this is important to him I try to honor it when I can. If it benefits my son and it keeps the peace between his father and I am here for it. It's a win-win. On the other hand, for me, Elias needs to brush his teeth after he eats sweets. This is in addition to the traditional times. Doing what you can to accommodate the other parent when appropriate only aides in your relationship as co-parents and benefits the child (ren). Things go along much smoother when we are working together because the stress and disagreements will come. Starting from a place of agreement and peace makes those disagreements a temporal thing that can be addressed with ease. You don't have to address conflict while in turmoil.

Again, speaking negatively, does very little to help you or your children, but it can be a barrier to the father/child relationship down the line. Who wants to be asked ten years from now, "why did you keep me from my father"? Lastly, it teaches a precious lesson to your child, positive or negative. Be careful!

- Establish clear boundaries! Accept what his role is and keep it that way. As with many things, situations may arise where you will need to give a little, and that's okay, but the "giving" cannot bring confusion, nor can it cross that boundary. If ever you run into some difficulty, look at the result. If the result is NOT what you want it to be, then that line or lines have been blurred.
- Acknowledge your own motives. So many times, people present their motives as they want them seen not as they are.

This will be very hard to have peace and to establish the partnership for the sake of the child if you are not honest going into this partnership! "How can any two walk TOGETHER unless they be agreed" (Amos 3:3).

- Make sure YOUR expectations and responsibilities are clear! Furthermore, they should be agreed upon and realistic. Do you expect the father of your children to do or buy things for you? If so, where would you draw the line? If not, why not?

These goals should not be different if you are still in a relationship with the father! A familiar saying right now is "play your position." I like the general feel of this saying. Imagine a football game. If the quarterback is out of position, how effective will he be in getting the ball down the field? Or what if you were the person catching the ball (aka the receiver) in the wrong spot? It could easily result in the other team scoring the ball. It is no different than it is here. If there is confusion about who does what or what should happen "in case" something else happens, it can lead to unnecessary drama, conflict.

If you are not still in a relationship with the other person, you may want to reach agreements around that as best you can. When will that other person be introduced? Do the parents have to meet the person first? When will the child be left alone with the new mate? Can the new mate discipline the child? Seek peace and agreement when you can. IF the co-parenting relationship is strong, then you will do better when it comes time to face some difficulty.

❦ 9 ❦

HI! IT'S WILLIAM'S MOM (ESTABLISHING YOUR OWN IDENTITY)

Who are you? How would you define YOU? Sitting where you are at this moment, how would you answer this question? As a young person, you are trying to determine who you are and going to be. I submit that becoming an adult; you know who you are and look to better it. Loosely defined, identity is the composite of attributes, skills, attributes, hobbies, and experiences that make you who you are. As of this book, I think that my identity is pretty established. I genuinely believe that who I am as a person and parent is set, but continues to be refined as I continue to live in this life. So why talk about identity? Why does it matter?

Your identity is being formed regardless of what you do or don't do. As you experience new things and take on new opportunities in life, who you are and will be is being formed. My call to action for you is to take an active role in that now. Yes, for you, but not ONLY for you. Part of your identity is a "parent." Once you decided you were having this baby, a new facet of your identity was formed. Which, in turn, will impact how you parent. Your identity will be comprised of the roles you hold and execute based on the beliefs and values you hold. If you are aren't as whole as you can be, how will you cultivate this in your child? I ask you this in establishing your own identity, just know that you will be a parent before you are a daughter/son or any other role. Being a young adult, so many people may try to define you from the outside looking in based on so many things they see about you. This can be a help or a hindrance when you are still figuring it out yourself.

It will more than likely be a chaotic world for you at this point because you are now thrown into an adult world, but you clearly are not an adult. If you are legally an adult, that's okay. This chapter is for you too! Overall, you are either coming into or becoming who you will be as an adult and a parent. Depending on who you ask, others may identify me as the "ice princess," a hard worker, aloof, or impulsive. While navigating all the aspects of who you are, and the roles you may have in society, you must maintain the most critical part of your identity, your role as a parent. These roles will always intersect. For instance, Deanna, the woman, the daughter, the sibling, and the friend will always cross with Deanna, the mother (a.k.a. William, Tallia, and Elias' mom).

I got so used to hearing the latter that I was thrown off when I heard my name! At daycare, my children were about two and three years old, respectively. The teachers referred to me as William and Tallia's mom. This was carried over at church, at school, and in the neighborhood. Before long, I wore this moniker with pride! I loved being *William and Tallia's* mom. It didn't take long for conflict to set in. As I matured and had more life experiences, I accepted that this was now my reality. Sometimes who I am as a woman may not jibe with who I am as a mother, yet I had a responsibility to nurture both sides. Yes, you do have that responsibility.

I am a holistically healed woman, and to be that woman requires work. As I began to engage in counseling and utilizing in the Bible, I begin to see things in myself that I had missed before. I began to see here's that I didn't connect with, and habits that I had or accepting some of the negative things I heard about myself were true. I am referred to by my family as an ice princess, being cold and very matter-of-fact. And that's okay. Now we're able to joke about it because I have used that opportunity to dig up the rude as to why I am the way that I am. I accepted who I was, but I wanted to know why? Why am I so-called cold?

Through some prayer, soul searching, and therapy, I determined a few things that contributed to that. One being, I was required to care for my younger brothers and sisters. We went to foster care several times, and during my last stint where I aged-out (stayed in foster care until I was 18), I learned a phrase that I would never forget. That phrase is a parentified child. Meaning I had the responsibilities of a parent! I was a parentified child. So yes, at times, I was cold as a person. I was bearing a lot. I had resentment and frustration often. I had a slew of emotions tied into those obligations that I did not acknowledge before. I acknowledge them now. I still feel like I have a way to go, but knowing that I am on this journey allows you to continue to evolve. And I want to continue to evolve. I want to be the best woman that I can be, and I can't do that without working through the things that make me who I am. Good, bad, or indifferent.

When I was younger, I was classified as a "fast" girl because I hung out with guys. I was a tomboy who also liked girly things. I didn't fit wholly to either the tomboy side or the girly side, which I honestly think is more common than I realized. Nevertheless, when I got pregnant, those who thought I was "fast" were convicted of that. Granted, they were wrong, but I understand now the APPEARANCE of my actions. In my subjective mind, I would challenge that thinking, but I can understand it to a degree. I looked the part by playing football, video games and play fighting. Then, girls didn't do these things, so in the minds of those who shared that opinion, the only logical explanation was I HAD to be having sex with all of them. It taught me an important lesson. I could retain *their perception* of who I was and live accordingly or define myself for myself. Deciding how to define yourself will impact you as you are cultivating your identity as a persona and subsequently as a parent. As the old saying that goes: *it's not what they call you, it's who you answer to*. Who are you answering to? What are you answering to?

Do you realize that you answer to yourself? Your identity starts and ends in your head so what are you saying to you? What are you saying about yourself to yourself? As a parent, I would be down on myself based on what I could give my children or even the mistakes that I made. I would refer to myself as a bad mother. This is negative talking. Of course, when you plant those seeds that grow into a belief, which then guides your actions. I became lax on things that I was strict on, allowing more sugar or more TV before the revelation that I was doing fine! I was 18 with two kids in a small apartment with very little support. At times, it was my cousin who was my only support. My children helped me to see how I was a better mom than I gave myself credit for. They never looked at me with contempt or disappointment. It forced me to ask myself why I am stating these things to myself? Once I stopped the negative talk, I was able to plan how to address the aspects of our life that I did not like.

Know that negative self-talk will never help you become that person you are meant to be. I have had to overcome this myself. As a social worker and a former foster child, I valued doing a good job. I hated the thought of doing paperwork. Although it was an essential part of my job, I held it as an optional part of my job. Part of my work identity became that I didn't do my paperwork timely. I was regarded as a mediocre worker in my mind. I had help in crafting this negative talk. I had a supervisor that no matter what I did, he appeared to look at me with disdain. When I messed up, I was made an example of, and when did well, I didn't hear anything. When I realized this was how I was looked at, I would be so hard on myself. The negative talk began to pick up steam in my head, furthering my negative thoughts to myself. I wanted to be seen as a person who was excellent, who cared about the kids and did their best work all the time. After all, that was my reputation at one time.

Working backward from that initial thought that I was a bad worker, I realized that initial thought had additional thoughts growing out of it. I began to feel like everyone was talking about me, that my boss didn't like me, and other things. I confronted Tom and ask him what did I do for him to feel this way towards me. I flatly asked him why didn't he like me. He was dumbfounded and stated he didn't feel anything towards me, and most certainly didn't have feelings of dislike for me. I was stunned. When he began to simply state that if he had any misgivings, they would be addressed, apologized for any role he may have played in this, and told me to speak to him again if I began to feel this way again. It was at this moment I realized how bad the negative thinking had become and the impact of it.

Why am I mentioning this to you? To encourage you to be mindful when crafting your identity. Whose report will you believe? I believe that you cannot produce something for your children or in your children that you do not have inside of you. As parents, we want our children to do great things to the best of their ability. I wanted my children to do everything I did and then everything I couldn't. I had to believe that was possible, and if I didn't see that for myself, I would not be able to cultivate that for my children. If I don't want my children to have a poverty mindset, I first must ensure that I don't have one.

Additionally, keeping this in mind as you go about your life will be helpful as you will undoubtedly have your parents, friends, and family weighing in your identity as a parent. This is hard for new parents who are adults. There is a phrase that has gained popularity lately. *Mom-shaming* is the art of shaming another woman's mothering. We all do things differently based on our culture, goals, and experiences. If who you are is on shaky or uncertain ground, how will it sustain arrows from all sides?

Take this opportunity to establish who you are. If you are unpleased in any area that is okay. These things are temporal and subject to change! Be open to it. Even now, with adult children, I still am refining who I am as continue to evolve into who I will be. Refining Deanna is something I enjoy because it usually results in my esteem being affirmed, confidence is boosted, and having a new experience. I was in a church one time, and the pastor says, "anything alive ought to be growing." That has always stuck with me. I know that growing is work. For me, I use that as an opportunity to challenge myself, to evaluate myself. If I find myself saying, "that's just how I am," I look at that and look and see if I am growing in that area. Establishing your identity is just that. But enjoy the journey. If I am stagnant, I figure out a way to challenge myself to grow beyond that to be a better me. My identity, as a mother or a person, is not going to be linked to being someone that I am generally unpleased with if I can help it.

As a mother, I would classify myself as "old-school." I associate with a lot of those values and ways of thinking. I pride myself on being a hybrid of the old and the new. An example of old-school parenting is no back-talk. I could not do it at all. When my parents spoke, there was not ever a discussion after. Asking a question for clarity after receiving an instruction had to be done in perfect timing, or my head could roll. Even as an adult, my mother still feels like on some things, her words need to be the final word! I am almost 40, and still, she feels that this is what is best. Granted, she has learned this not realistic, so she accepts that her word is no longer the law in my life, but if she could still do that, she would.

As a new-school parent, I want my children to be heard. I want them to practice having a voice and knowing that it matters. How will I do my best to make sure they are doing this outside of the house if they never get to practice inside the house? For me, the time for this is when you are asked. If they want to discuss their feelings or understanding later, they can come back to me to discuss it. My parents would never have done that! For me, I like my children to understand why I am doing things, so my rationale is usually known to them. In my experience, it helps them carry out my direction, even when they don't agree. I do not feel I owe them an explanation, but if in my life, they are not able to identify why I am doing something and want clarity, I may consider having that conversation with them. With that, though, *because I said so* still is a complete sentence with no explanation needed. My kids know at this point, there is typically no discussion after this sentence. With them being adults, I rarely use it, but it is in my arsenal. For better or for worse. So much so that as an adult, my daughter asked me why do parents say that. I told her I would answer this question generally. I told her that as parents, we see the big picture and know things, they may not be privy to in their role as my kids. If they trust me, it should be without question. Asking her if she trusted me, she stated she did and nodded, walking away, satisfied.

Who you are and who your children are is a part of your identity, your "brand?" Get busy branding! How do you brand your identity?

- What do you want to be known for as a person? As a parent? Start with this. This will be a guiding principle as you go forward.
- Identify who you are now, as much as you can. All of what you have experienced, what you like, what skills you possess, and personal attributes all contribute to your identity. Establishing a foundation will be helpful as you move forward. Watch that growth!
- Know that you are in control of your narrative, so watch what you say. Yes, even in your head.
- Be forward-thinking. Think of who you are impacting your children. Would you be proud of them following in your footsteps or following the plan you laid out for them?
- Give yourself space to evolve!

10

THE IMPORTANCE OF BEING FUTURE-MINDED; WHEN PREPARATION MEETS OPPORTUNITY.

Writing this title, I giggled a little as I can hear one of my former clients saying, "we wouldn't say it like that... we'd say, 'what that future do though' "? This is a tricky question in and of itself! On top of that, now you are making this decision to enter college while parenting, if not still pregnant. In my opinion, this a tiered question. If the answer is to enroll, the next step is what needs to happen so that you can apply? What are the barriers and possible solutions? Once you have the yes, the next tier is how do I do this as a parent? Depending on the age of the child that will determine "how" you go about doing this. You will hear and have heard me say a lot that we need to know what your needs are. The reason for this is straightforward. If your needs are not met, you will not be able to focus on any other task until it is met, including meeting the needs of your child. I know many of you will say, as I have said, that I will always meet my child's needs. Amen! I ask that are you satisfied with meeting them just to say you met them, or do you want to meet them fully? I was speaking to someone who congratulated me on buying a house for my children. My attitude was one of dismissiveness and indifference. She asked me why I felt that way. I told her very frankly that I don't need a pat on the back for what I am "supposed to do." She smiled and thought for a minute. She asked me why I bought the house. I quickly responded to my children. She said, why do you cook lasagna for your son or cheesecake for your daughter? I paused to look at her incredulously, and I said that I cook them for my children because they love them. She replied and stated, "exactly." I stared at her, completely missing a point that is so obvious to me now! She said, "You would have met their needs with a bologna sandwich! You could have stayed in your apartment, and your kids would have been fine! They would have been FED and HOUSED, but you wanted to meet their needs in a way that satisfies. Satisfying to both you and them"! Wow! Now I ask you, if you are not meeting your needs, how can you meet the needs of your child in a way that they are satisfied? How about you? If that is your goal, you must be aware of what your needs are and how to, effectively, meet them without infringing on the needs of your child. All of that rests on having preparation and planning. That will allow for clarity of mind and thought!

So how does that relate in deciding to go to college? You can't make a sound decision with other things stealing your attention in your life, aka having your needs go unmet! For instance, if you need to study, and you began to get hungry, you may go a little while without needing a snack or even choose to overlook those familiar hunger pangs. Once several hours have gone by, your attention and motivation would then begin to shift to getting that food and alleviating that pain. It is no different when assessing enrolling in school. To be successful, you have to have your needs mostly, if not entirely, met. That "entirely" could mean different things depending on the individual.

It's never too late to think ahead. Start to identify what you want to do in your life within the next year. For some individuals, it is not college, or it's not college right now. Don't feel pressure to come up with big or societal driven goals. College is a societal norm. Society his deemed automatic enrollment into college as at the automatic and normal response. Society tells us this is the expected timeline, and that is what you should be doing after graduation from high school to be successful. What I'm telling you is your life is up starting over. Be future-minded. If future-minded for you means college great. If not? Great.

You can decide what you do next. If you have not graduated high school, do you want to get your GED, or do you want to finish High School? Look at what each of those things need. Look at what you will be required to do under each of those options. Yes, I'm telling you to write it out. Even if it's on the same sheet of paper. Write heading as a GED and the other heading as finish High School. I know there are Community Schools that can help you both get your high school diploma and get your GED. You have to list everything that is required of you so that you can truly make an informed decision. Think of everything that you would have to do down to the daycare. Believe me, the more prepared you are, the easier your plan will be.

Once you have identified what you want to do with your life in the next year then, we look at the list and identify any barriers to achieving these goals. So, you are getting a GED. What is the barrier? Maybe you don't have help to get around. What can we do to help you with that? Who can you call? Is there a bus route that goes to your hair?? Are you able to Uber? These are things that we have to examine. Knowing what you want to do helps you identify the barriers to what you want to do, and once you have those barriers identified, guess what? They can be removed.

Take the time to cry, feel down, or pout. Just don't stay there. The next day is a new day and a new opportunity. Keep at it.

Utilize the support you have or find help to put around you. Remember, support does not have to be a mother, father, sister, or friend. Anything or anyone dependable can count as support. I found community resources and utilized them as needed to get me to where I need to be. You never know what can come of it. You may cry. You may feel down. You may be sad but just know. And support does not have to be a mother or father or sister or cousin in the fridge. If you genuinely feel that you don't have any of these things, then we can try to find resources in the community, and you may have to do stuff alone that's okay. I'm not saying that it's not hard because it is, but what I don't want you to feel is defeated and what I don't want you to feel is alone. We can get through this we can get through this together. Allow me to tell a story about preparation.

I had been struggling on the bus. I was then in nursing school. My book bag weighed 30 pounds with a two and three-year-old walking or on my hip. We had crossed the bridge, and I had groceries, my backpack, and my babies crossing through 3 inches of snow. Traffic quickly whizzed by me, further driving the wind past me angrily in many different directions. That day I prayed as I had never prayed before. I simply needed a car! During this time in my life, I was a Christian. I attended church all day every day. The church that I attended at the time had been teaching that you have not or you ask amiss (or outside the will of God). At church the next day, the pastor stated we could just ask God, and He would provide what you need. He would prepare the answer. He ministered how, when the man in the bible had prayed instantly, the Lord dispatched the answer (forgive me, I am paraphrasing). During my internship, I had been praying and walking like those walking around the wall of Jericho. After I was done, God told me to call and ask around for my car. Someone was going to give it to me. I know that sounds crazy. I would not believe it either if I didn't drive off in it later!

I asked around and was told no several times. I stopped feeling defeated and foolish, but when you know that this is what the Most High would ask you to do. I picked up the phone again and called a church. This time I wasn't told no. I wasn't scoffed at. I was told to hold on. They took my information and said she would call me back. I hung up and instantly began to praise God. I know I didn't have the keys in my hand, but I felt in my spirit that I knew this was it. I began to ask God what I wanted. I wanted it to be white, at least the heat working, a good radio, and I didn't want to have to put very much work into it. I wanted four doors so people could get in and out of my car without someone having to get out. I also wanted to be able to put my children in the car easier. Lord, I was ready for this car.

I received a callback, and I was told that someone was coming to visit me. I set the appointment, thanked her, got off the phone, and praised God. I continued to glorify God and blessed Him. Once we got the appointment, a nice older man called me and asked if I had my driver's license, and I confirmed that I did. He stated he wanted to have me meet the following day. I offered to meet him at the community college I attended. The next day was waiting where we agreed, and I was early! He arrived in a white car, and I prayed, thanking God for the car I would receive. The kind man asked me if I wanted to drive and I told him I did. I drove him to the DMV. *I know that he wanted to see me drive, but what is this?* I thought. I waited patiently and prayed. Thanking God that one day he may be the person God uses to provide me my car. In my head, I alternated between praying and praising god. The man then asked me to join him at the window.

"Do you have your ID, Deanna"? he asked politely.

"Yes, I do..." Slowly realizing what was happening. I presented my ID, signed the title, and the transaction was complete. He asked if I could continue driving, and I nodded, unable to speak. Silently, I prayed prayers of gratitude. As we approached his offices, the elder explained the events surrounding me getting my car. He stated the day I called a woman had brought in a vehicle to donate to the church. The only stipulation was that it had to go to a person who needed it, preferably a woman with kids. He wanted to see me drive and only had one more request; drop him off at the office. I happily obliged and openly began to praise God. The elder started to agree as I pulled up to his office. He shook my hand, wished me best of luck, and departed, leaving me to sit in my blessing. I drove away, and I didn't know which emotion would feel, but I seemed to feel every happy emotion I could. I pulled over and got out to see what God had done. I jumped out, leaving the door open to see the car that I had prayed for. The white car, four doors, radio, and heat were working with no work to put in. Now I am sitting in my blessing. I wholly believe that I can sit in my blessing because I first set in my PREPARATION. I had positioned myself to receive it! I had learned how to drive, obtained my Driver's License, learned about the general care of cars. I was ready.

From that short interaction, not only did I get a car, but I met a family that I still maintain contact with to this day! All of this was born from that community resource! Listen, if you truly feel that you don't have any of these things, then we can try to find support in the community, and you may have to do stuff alone that's okay. I would never say it would not be hard because it is and was for me. It is doable. Whether you go to school or get a job, we know that you have to make money. You can always go back to school if you decide to get a job first. You could take a class at a time. You could go to school and do work-study for income. You could get your GED, as I did, and work full time. There is a way, and with proper planning and supports, you will find it.

Here's your homework:

- Set your goals. Short term to long term. These goals will change, so don't be afraid to adjust them as needed! Set immediate goals (one week, two weeks, a month, three months, a year, and five years) for school.
- Identify barriers to you being successful in college! Part of being successful is planning! Acknowledge the barriers to achieving your goals so that you have ample opportunity to plan to address them.
- IF you go to college, meet with an advisor to see if any credits can transfer and to have an established plan to get enrolled and going in school. Do not be afraid to meet periodically or as needed with that advisor. They are there to help you, so let them help. If you go, you need to complete your FAFSA (Free Application for Federal Student Aid). This will determine the amount of aid you will receive. Try not to take out any loans. IF you go to college, plan out your monthly bills so that you can see where the money needs to go so any overages can go to your bills. This will ensure your needs are met, which will allow you to focus on your work.
- In keeping with the planning motif, let's plan for the degree you'd like and life after it. For instance, don't seek to get a degree in social work making 30,000 a year but leaving college with 60,000 + in loans! College will last for 4 to 6 years for

undergrad, but you are a mother for LIFE! Don't put yourself in debt and limit how you can provide for your children.

- If you don't enroll in college, your goals still need to be set that were identified in the first part of this checklist.
- Looking at your goals, identify how you would make money to support you and your family. Don't lean on family and friends. At any given moment, that could change, and then you will be at a loss. IF they help you, that is great. IF they don't, you didn't plan on it, so it cannot cost you.
- What do you want to do with your life? What is required to achieve that? Do you want to be an artist? A musician? What needs to happen so that goal can be met? How will the needs of your family be met while you are working toward that goal?
- Lastly, reassess those supports! If you need new ones, that is okay and if they are still in place even better! Lean on them. You will need them, even if this it's "just" to give you a pep talk or purchase notebook paper.

11

AN ADVOCATE IN ALL THINGS (EVEN WHEN THE BEST DECISION MAY NOT ALWAYS BE THE EASIEST) - THE ADVOCACY GAME.

As of the writing of this book, there is a top-rated show that I love or am slightly addicted to. It is called *The Blacklist*. It is everything I need it to be! There is a character called Raymond "Red" Reddington. He is the epitome, the very example of an advocate, all though not in a traditional sense. The show's premise is that Red has a list that is much more dangerous than the FBI's Top Ten. Why? Because they are such a low profile that the FBI doesn't even know that they exist! Red broker's a deal with the FBI to remain out of jail AND still conduct his criminal business in exchange for the names on this list. In essence, he has advocated for what he feels is in his best interests. You may be wondering why I would bring this up? Red was able to go to the people who could impact his life. For the good or the bad, and advocate for his needs to be met.

Through his advocacy, he ensured he would be protected by the FBI from his enemies. He would not be arrested for the crimes committed and maintaining the authority to pick which *Blacklister* (or a person on the blacklist) he could give them in exchange for what he wanted. He identified what his needs were, outlined a plan, and subsequent action steps to work this plan and negotiated the terms until he got what he needed. He was able to advocate, or fight, for himself.

In one of the episodes, Red was in a sketchy situation with an FBI agent. He told the agent what needed to happen, and the agent hesitated, stating that they were unsure that Red was making a sound decision for them. Do you know what Red's response was? He said, "I'll always do what's in my best interest, and that's a man that you can trust." That's the way we have to look at our care and meeting our needs.

When you can be a strong advocate for yourself, you will always have at least one person on your side, and that will always be enough! Who would you trust to decide if you needed surgery? Or, if you have an issue in your body, who could explain it more adequately than you? That's what he is saying. He knows what his needs are and will ALWAYS make decisions that will be in his favor. Let's do a quick evaluation of ourselves. Let's consider your life; spirit, soul, and body. Let's suppose that you are the CEO of your life and answer these questions:

- How strong are you in identifying what you need and why you need it?
- Do you feel you can look at the *endgame* or the longer-term impact of a decision you are making today?
- What if you are told no for something you feel like you need? How would you handle it?
- If you are missing information, where do you get it?
- Do you trust your ability to find out what information you should have BEFORE you make your decision?
- Are you aware, keenly aware, that what is going on with your body? Your baby? And that you can advocate for what you need. You deserve to be listened to.

If you do not see more "yeses" than "no's," your advocacy game may need to be stepped up! You should always be able to trust YOU. You are the first person to see when and how things are going, good or bad. You are ALSO the first person to be affected by how things are going, good or bad. So being able to advocate for yourself is essential. It's hard if you do not have anyone to bounce ideas off of. Even the smartest and most grounded person can benefit from that. But, if you don't have that at this time, that's ok! It just means that you will need to be able to do it, and that is scary! Being afraid or uncomfortable is okay, but do not let those nerves disarm you from asking the questions that need to be asked and demanding the answers that you need. This skill will come in handy for yourself and your children!

Try not to be intimidated by the person you are speaking to when advocating for your needs. A little while ago, I had a Chrysler PT Cruiser. The car is no longer made today (I can believe it). It was a very temperamental car, and it was ALWAYS expensive to fix because of how the engine was stacked in the vehicle. Every repair started at $500.00. In any event, I took my car to this mechanic when it was overheating. He "fixed" my car enough. We took it and was running with it and then it started doing the same thing. I called him and asked him why my car was doing this after he fixed it. He told me he could look at it again...for a fee. I told him that I paid him to FIX the car... not rig the vehicle so that it would roll off of his lot. I took it to another dealer who told me I needed a new timing system, which was what the first mechanic was supposed to have fixed. I went back to the first mechanic, who told me to shove off. I called a consumer support service to address it, and he stated that he would fix it again...for a price. I had to go to court and sue this man. All through the process, he was trying to get me to settle, despite me knowing what was right. In the end, I won in court, and you would think that would be over, but of course, it was not. I had to take him back to court and set up a payment plan to get my money. He fought me tooth and nail, but that did not deter me.

With that, I encourage you not to be deterred. It is sickening to fight. It is disturbing to have to defend yourself, especially in a situation you shouldn't have to or to someone you may feel like you shouldn't have to, but if it's necessary? It's necessary. Do what you have to do. Even a fight where you are the right-side in. Having to fight, having someone or something coming against you does not indicate that what you are advocating for is wrong! It just means you will have to be persistent in seeking what is right for you!

- Evaluate your ability to advocate. 0 being - I can't advocate at all. 10 being - *I can advocate for YOU if I need to)*.
- Stay the course. Know what you want and be committed to it. If you don't know what you want, you will not be able to advocate for it.
- Don't be afraid to be rejected! Press until you can't anymore.
- Practice your game face. If you look easily dismissible, you will be.
- Begin with the end in mind. When you get tired or want to give up, think about why you started advocating in the first place.
- Be in the right! I always teach those I mentor to "operate from a position of strength." You can't go hard if you are wrong.

❧ 12 ❧

RELATIONSHIPS... AM I ALLOWED?

A Relationship at any age is an involving journey. As a parent, you may feel like you don't have space for a relationship. I had a young mother ask me if she was "allowed" to have a relationship. Her child was 18 months, and she had begun to have the stirrings of wanting to be in a relationship. I told her that she is allowed, of course. Having a relationship and connection with someone is normal! What I loved is, she was taking the time to see that this was the right decision. Gone are the days when mothers would sneak and have their relationships entirely away from their children, or at least it should be. I am not advocating for parents to disregard all decorum when it comes to dating because they have a right to happiness. What I am suggesting is a measured approach.

I was watching a show called *Blackish*. On the show, Dre was shocked to find out his mother had relationships while he was younger. He held her as a good mother because he couldn't recall her entering into any relationship, only being devoted to him. Entering a relationship as a parent, especially a new parent, there is a lot that comes with that. You are now exposing yourself, your children, and all of your futures to this new person. I would submit that is not a decision that one enters into lightly. Depending on where you are in your life, I would genuinely encourage you to examine the timing and rationale for entering into a new external relationship. Are you a young adult, or are you a teenager? Are you in college or working? Are you still processing trauma, or are you trucking along, okay? Regardless of your answer to these questions, the question I feel any person needs to answer when contemplating entering into a new relationship is simple. *Why do I want this relationship?* It is imperative to identify the reason you desire a relationship. From that question, more will emerge as you evaluate the pros and cons of this decision. What are you hoping to gain? Assistance? Support? Additionally, what can you offer? Any healthy relationship will be an exchange! Going into a relationship will require something of you! Are you at a place where you have extra to give? Lastly, are you a healthy and whole person?

So many times, I have seen individuals seek relationships as if that is what is missing from their life! As if they are nothing without having a mate, a "bae." If we were to look at their behaviors and how they carried themselves when it came to the absence of a relationship, they GIVE the impression they feel incomplete as a single person. They mourn the absence of that mate or uses that to evaluate their worth as a mate. Let's take a step back, particularly on a day when you are emotionally, mentally, spiritually, and physically strong, and examine the prospect of a new relationship.

First and foremost, you have to look at how they will impact your child (ren). Secondly, do not buy into the notion that you are *entitled* to a relationship when *you* see fit. Your children are your most important priority. When you became a parent, you decided that you are no longer the most important person in your world. Everything must be running through the filter of *how will this affect my child??* Will the relationship take you away from your child? How will it add to the lives of your family AND you as a person? Don't MAKE the relationship make sense. Truth does not have to be reasoned; it has to be accepted. Don't compromise your child, their future, or the relationship with your child to have a mate. Please know the person will come in time.

As of this book, I am in my late 30's, and I have had five boyfriends. Some of them were when I was younger. Most people, if not all, have had at least one relationship that "had they waited" something could have been different.

The one relationship I wish I had waited on was boyfriend number 4. I met him when I was about 20 years old. We met in the weirdest way, but that is neither here nor there. He was not wholly a person that I would have picked for myself, but I was curious about learning more about him. He was a friend of my younger brother. He continued to come around, and before you know it? He was asking my brothers' permission to date me. If we can gloss over the fact that he was asking my brothers' permission to date me, I was relieved when he finally decided to approach me.

I knew that he liked me, and I was tired of keeping people at bay. One night I had a game/card night at my house. That was quite common. We played until we were tired and then everyone just crashed. This night he stayed over and decided to stay up with me in the kitchen while I cleaned up. I never finished that night as we stayed up the whole night talking. He was the first person who was not a therapist who sincerely asked about some of the things I had gone through. The more I talked, the more time spun on, carrying us toward the morning. He sat intrigued and transfixed, marveling at what I shared. He looked at me and said, "I will never let anyone hurt you again."

I can remember how vulnerable and excited I was at this moment. When he said those words to me, I breathed them in. They were cloaked in honesty and sincerity. I found myself zoning out and realizing that I was slipping from bored and curious to liking. Lord, I was starting to like this boy! I wanted to like him, and more importantly, I was happy that he would be there for me. He reached his hand across the table and began to make promises speaking directly to my brokenness. I glanced around my apartment, looking for any opportunity to distract myself from him. It wasn't working. My eyes looked down at the 1950's table I had received as a donation. The stains in the melamine were pronounced and allowed me to focus on something else to regain myself. I was grateful that he couldn't see my true emotions. Inside, my thoughts fought to remain in my brain. I held his hand and said, "Is that right"? He nodded factually. He began to talk, allowing me time to regain complete composure. Or so I thought. I knew it was bad. I felt like I was all in. And I was.

In this relationship, I sincerely fell in love. I can say now that I tried hard to make it work. In hindsight, that was the first clue that I should have waited; I was trying too hard! I felt that this time, I needed to stay and do something different to make this work. I had committed my life to the Lord. So, it was easy to push people away with that as the guise. Once I began to stray from the things of God, I began to entertain men. I used them as a fourth for spades with my cousin and myself. I let them treat me or take me out and more but never entered into a relationship. When anything came up that I didn't like, I would leave. I was determined to change that, and I figured with someone so seemingly protective was a great practice dummy. I could list out all of the lessons this relationship has taught me, but I will instead focus on one: how to take a punch from a man.

Granted, by NO means am I saying that you will enter into an abusive relationship! What I AM saying is that if I would have waited to spare my children having to see me grabbed, smacked, choked, or worse, I should have. I often state that I very rarely regret things that I have had to endure. Rarely. They have made me who I am today and that woman I can truly appreciate. If I am honest, I did not give much thought to the questions that I am asking you to ask yourself before entering into a relationship.

Don't get me wrong, I **did** ask how this would affect my children, and I was able to justify it in my mind. I only saw benefits with no **MAJOR** drawbacks. That was another sign to me that was not looking at a potential relationship with the most objective mindset. Sure, it was exciting, fun, and flattering. We waited nine months to have sex. For me, that was not a long time, but I was so flattered that we were both seeing to save ourselves. It kept me in the relationship. He was a preacher's kid, so he was on board with not fornicating. Every other guy I met was okay with my abstinence until they realized what that involved, real abstinence! Then they would either leave the relationship or tell me that they would have to "get it from somewhere else," certainly wrapping things up for me.

Now I wanted to prove to myself that I could do it. I could stay. That is what I did. I committed to this man and before you knew it? We were a "family." If he got home first, he would have the kids at the table doing homework and starting dinner. His parents were supportive and welcoming. We went over to his family's home for dinners, went to his parents' church together, and more. He was a member of my family, as well. It was going okay together until it wasn't.

I was so busy doing what I needed; it was lost on me that I did not require much of him. Once I did, that is when the trouble began. When he wasn't able to provide what he needed, he grew more and more insecure. My blessings continued to come. This fed his jealousy or envy of me. I learned after I was out of the relationship. I decided I was done. I wanted out and sat him down to tell him. He refused to leave. He grew angry, and his drinking increased as did the darkness around him. I would put my foot down, and I would leave. He would threaten me, rough me up, and then I'd end up back with him. This cycle continued for years. I would love to come home and see three gift sets of full Victoria's Secret perfume sets, each held in place by a cute teddy bear and Hallmark card with nothing but flowery words. I decided to try again, hoping it would be better, but it wasn't. I stayed for long for several reasons. I was hopeful. I felt bad for him, and when things were going well, I liked what we were. None of those reasons are reasons to stay.

To top it off, he was the purported black sheep of his family. From almost the beginning, he told me stories of how his sister was favored, and he was mistreated. He told me how his mother often told him that she wished she had had an abortion with him. He knew how to get me. Sadly, between the love I had for him and being empathetic was all it took. Just like that, I was back in. I knew what it was like to be left by a loved one. It was hard to inflict that wound on him. I decided that I would endure until I could getaway. My plan was working well until one night, he wanted affection, and I wasn't feeling it. When he asked me, I told him why I wasn't affectionate. I simply stated to him, "I don't want you here." In his injury, he said something disrespectful to me. As I was walking away, I dismissed him, telling him to go to hell. Instinctively he threw a plate at me. He ran in the front room, and I stood, refusing to be scared.

"Why you act like you ain't scared of me? You ain't a man. I'll fuck you up".

"Why would I be scared of you? Don't throw anything at me again. Like I said,". I looked past his shoulder to my children, watching intense anticipation. I sighed. *Girl, it is not worth it. Just forget it.* I thought to myself. As I refocused on his intention to try and quell the situation, he poked me in my forehead so hard that I lost both my footing and my cool. I then tripped into my tv stand behind me. My resignation was replaced with rage. I slapped him, and he hit me back. I began to try to fight him but be bear-hugged me and ran me 5 feet across my living room into a wall.

"Mom,"! My children yelled out from the hall stairs as they got out of the way. I wrestled to get free but was no use. I was done.

"Tallia! William! Go to the car. I am coming. We are leaving!" My son stood transfixed. My daughter grabbed my son and ran out. My son came back in, and my daughter followed. I yelled for my son and daughter to leave. Again, I watched my daughter make it through the door. My son was slower to move, wanting to protect me. I yelled again, and he relented, making his way to the door. My boyfriend was not having it and tried to close the door. My son was at the door. Although he didn't appear to be hurting him, I didn't want him to and kneed my boyfriend in the face. He dropped his hold on the door, shifting his focus to me, allowing my son to run. I yelled for them to get in the car because I knew what was coming.

As quickly as the words left my mouth, my expectation was met. My "protector" had once again punched me in the face, sending me flying into the wall. I can still remember hearing the thermostat shatter as I hit on my way to the floor. I staggered up and into the kitchen as his threats followed me, where I grabbed the knife. Seeing this be backed up enough for me to get in the car. He ran, trying to keep us from leaving the parking lot. He pleaded with me, screaming he was sorry.

My children were screaming for me to get away, and I was trying my hardest to quiet all of the noise so that I could drive. Finally, I had gotten the Oldsmobile cleared of the parking spot and him. I felt I was home free, and he did too. As a last-ditch effort, he punched the window of the car. Although it was the rear passenger side, the glass hit me in the driver seat as I struggled to shift between gears. I stopped to make sure my children were alright. He left for a while, but he would be back.

I decided it was over, and the next day I would get the apartment complex to make him leave. To my surprise, he had every right to be there as I did. I was being told by my landlord that, "if I put him out, I will have to put you out." Really?! Now I get home to more presents, more flowers, and more apologies. I was defeated. What was my great idea? *Since we have to be here, maybe we can try to make it work?* The reality? It would be a matter of time that the abuse would escalate. And it did. Resulting in us fighting in a car on a major road, resulting in a bruised eye, chin, jaw, and ear as well as other injuries.

I was not ready to entertain this relationship or any relationship for that matter! I have seen so much, but the concept of love and relationships was flawed. I was not experienced nor trained in that area. Furthermore, I had not examined *why* I wanted this relationship. I needed to be healed. I felt so many times in my life before I was not protected, and he provided that. I was not ready to give much to him because I had not addressed my brokenness. I have heard it said that a woman who is trying to leave a domestic violence situation has to do so seven times. I can say this is true. If I had taken my time, I could have seen him for whom he was. I could have spared myself and, most importantly, my children, tons of grief. Again, that relationship taught me *so* much, but the lesson was a costly one!

Your experience may not be as grave as mine. Still, being able to give of yourself requires you to be in a place to give it. It can be something seemingly simple as patience or setting and enforcing boundaries. Whatever you have to offer is easier to do as a whole person. It also provides you with your best shot at having a healthy and mutually beneficial relationship.

The last thing I want to leave you with is: Whoever is for you is who you are choosing for your children. Just because they are in a relationship with you does not mean they will share in the love and provision for your children. Red flags should be deal-breakers. Don't push past those!

If you do feel this is the right time to begin a new relationship, consider the following:

- Can it wait? If not, why not?
- What do you hope to gain out of the relationship?
- What are your immediate, short term, and long-term goals, and how does that relationship play into achieving those goals?
- What do you plan to give to the person and the relationship?
- What will need to change for the relationship to occur?
- IF all your needs are met, would you still want this person? In a relationship?
- Are you willing to move slowly into the relationship?
- Are you staying open to identifying red-flags?
- Are you able and willing to remove yourself from the relationship based on one or more of these red flags?
- Am I a good woman to myself? Am I a good man to myself? You have to be a good woman to yourself or the man to yourself before you can be a good man or a good woman to someone else. This has to be your goal. Consider how this will affect your child and both of your lives.

13

MOVING FORWARD!

Insert your name here! It will be easy to get lost in the numerous roles and responsibilities that are present in your life. You are a child, possibly a sibling, hopefully still a student amongst so many other things. To top that all off, you are now a parent. A role that is arguably the most important and equally tricky role you find yourself in. This chapter is meant to serve as a launching pad for ideas and strategies that you can resort back to when you feel you are lost, alone, or confused.

Here, I share what skills and strategies I utilized to get me to the next goal as I pressed on, moving forward. Write a letter to yourself to set up reminders of things you'd like to do as well as the victories you have enjoyed. Again, this is necessary as you navigate the sea of life. All of your varying roles may engulf you at times. I pray this chapter will serve as a springboard when you get down on yourself. Let it serve as a manifesto for you to move forward. Let it serve to encourage you to see where you have come from. Even if it's just "mental growth" to stop and acknowledge that growth will only serve to build you up. Here are a few things that really helped me along the way...

1. Affirmations

2. Planning it out
3. Writing it down

I mentioned, I found God early, and He helped me. He helped me so much. Often times, I will write a prayer or a letter to God. Quietly talking to Him from my heart. This is usually when I'm in a place where I could not speak, but I needed to "say something."

> *Lord, here I am again.*
>
> *Sitting here in a familiar pew, in a familiar place feeling very un-familiar.*
>
> *Peculiar.*
>
> *Tired again. Trying to get that old thing back, but I am unsure. I'm weary.*
>
> *Waves of emotion continue to crash beneath this stoic and calm exterior.*
>
> *This ability is creating a shell.*
>
> *True feelings and vulnerability are becoming buried in mistrust and a betrayal by you.*
>
> *My hallelujahs used to belong to you; ringing high in the heavens are now the syllables are strewn about the threshing floor.*
>
> *A new brokenness yet very old. I've been here before. When you've loved the unlovable and stood with the weak to find yourself standing alone with hurt so easily hurled to me. I don't want to feel this way anymore. I want to succeed. I want to feel safe. I want to be happy. I want to know you're real. But I guess in all of this, I praise you. I praise you. I praise you. I want to know there is a purpose for what you have allowed. Help. Me.*

For me, standing on His word and speaking that same word into my life kept me. Even if you are not religious, as the world would say, it has been proven that there is power in words. There is this whole resurgence of "affirmations," and there is a reason for that. They work. They are creative, on several levels. Affirming yourself is very beneficial, especially when you do not have someone affirming you already. Whether you do have someone or not being able to affirm yourself to yourself will carry you far. You will not always have access to a parent, to a pastor or a significant other. You have to stand on your own two feet and being able to affirm yourself? Priceless. That means if no one else has you? It will STILL be alright because YOU have you!

Planning it out and writing it out go hand in hand. The bible says to "write the vision and make it plain." This says a mouth full for me. Again, you don't have to approach this from a religious standpoint. Even removing the spiritual component, these tools will work for you. I am a visual learner. Writing out my plans and my goals aid me in seeing exactly where I am and what I still need to do. It also removes or limits any overthinking or emotionality that will not help you when you are making your plan. Planning as much as possible ensures that you can put things in place to accomplish the goals you set. When planning, you have to look at the entire picture, the good and the bad. If you can plan for the bad, it won't be a significant setback as you are going on your journey.

1. Conquer that thought life! An example I often give in my speeches is that you are running this race. You have to be as strong as possible to win, right? Having a negative or defeated self-life is akin to shooting yourself in the foot and then taking off yet wondering why you can't win the race!

2. Face your fears. Avoiding the things that give you pause will not resort in a win for you. Do it scared! Whatever IT is? Do it afraid. Face it and do it anyway. For me, I have found myself giving myself this speech. A fear I have had to face was the fear of failing. I would want something so bad, but that same desire would freeze me in my tracks. I would want to be successful and would overthink it, and before you knew it, I had not moved toward meeting that goal. At some point, you will be at a strategic inflection point. You will have to decide between bowing down from attacking a target because of whatever fear you have, or you will acknowledge that fear and press toward that goal. I quit my career to focus on my books, my speaking, and other businesses that I feel stirring around in my belly. I was afraid of failing because of what that meant to me. To quit my job and to now

accomplish the goals that lead me to quit would mean I quit for nothing! I am the provider for my family, and I am taking a step back to bet on myself. Now you are reading that book! I know what it means to be afraid, and I tell you to do it anyway. Make sure nothing is feeding your fear that may have an answer so that the fear could be alleviated. Once that is done? DO IT!

3. Define your character and integrity to which you can hold yourself accountable. Have you ever heard the phrase, "If you don't stand for something, you will fall for anything"? If you don't define yourself as hard-working? Diligent? You could easily fall victim to procrastination or anything else that is contrary to what you have planned for you and your child's life.

4. Admit your mistakes! This will carry you far in life. You will see that to you as a parent. As a child, you may even identify with this. I know I do! As a child, when a child looks you in their parents' face and lies, that is more damaging, especially when you can clearly see that they're lying? I genuinely believe that it is more upsetting than whatever they were trying to cover up in the first place (in most cases). That is no different for you. You want to be able to admit your mistakes so that you can go past it. You cannot change what you don't admit to.

5. Practice acceptance of things you cannot change. You will come across things that are out of your control, things that you have no understanding of why they are the way that they are. But you cannot change them. The only thing that you can do is change how you react to it. And the more time you spend thinking about why this is the way that it is? You're not spending any time or coming up with a solution to remove that obstacle or barrier. You are not operating from a position of strength.

6. Speaking of which, operate from a place of strength. This is a necessary skill. There's a reason for that. When you operate from a "strong place," the outcome will be great and will be quicker. For instance, let's say you were fighting Floyd Mayweather. Regardless of what you think of him as a person, we have to acknowledge that he is an accomplished boxer. Nevertheless, if you were to go into a match

with him, what is the first thing you would do? TRAIN! You would do that to ensure that you had the skills to beat him. You would make sure what you are putting into yourself is proper fuel for your mind, soul, and body. (here that would be akin to empowering thoughts, setting goals and utilizing affirmations) to yield you the results you want. You would undoubtedly lift weights. You would use these things to prime you for the battle. You would want to be in the best condition to do that, as strong as you can all the way around. To be victorious, we have to know what our weaknesses are and why they make us weak. If we know what is weakening us, we fix it to ensure that we win. We want the victory! Identifying what weakens us is not always easy, but it is still necessary.

Most people don't like to think about what weakens them because they have to admit a weakness. And there are various reasons that some may not want to be seen as weak or something don't like the vulnerability. Either way, you have to know and identify it to fix it! Once you do, you will be surprised at how quickly it can be removed and how much stronger you felt having overcome that obstacle or barrier.

7. Celebrate your victories. Yes, even the small ones. I cannot tell you how life can easily make you forget. It is incredibly empowering to look back on the barriers you have overcome, especially when you are looking at a new mountain.

8. Speaking of mountains, set goals for yourself and identify barriers to meeting those goals

9. Be mindful of your time. Count it as precious. I have learned that being polite may not always be the best thing. If someone is taking your energy or they are putting you in a negative headspace, there is absolutely nothing wrong with excusing yourself from their presence. You also have to be planful with your time. Yes, it may be fun to go out kicking it today, but if you don't have time tomorrow to rest and you have a busy evening, then Sunday, you don't have time to rest and have an active Sunday before you know it; it is the beginning of the workweek, and you have not had any time for you and, more

importantly, time for your baby. You are at your best for your baby when you are at your best. So be mindful of your time.

10. Know that you will miss the mark. Know that it is okay. Forgive yourself early, thoroughly, and often!

Bottom line - I want you to know that you can do this. I want you to remember to come away from this book; you can still be and do everything that you saw yourself doing before your pregnancy. It may be harder. It probably will be because now you are a young person who is now a parent. I want you to know that I have overcome so much in my life. As I sit here writing this book and thinking back, I can recollect all that I have overcome. I may even write another book about it :-), but I want you to know anything you have envisioned is doable. I spoke about affirmations and writing everything out, as those two things have been instrumental in my success. I truly believe that they are why I possess a sane mind and a healthy body at this point.

Again, this stemmed from my relationship with The Most High God. But these skills are not relocated only to those who are going to church. Try them (and other suggestions in this book) tweaking them to make them work for you. Tailor any information you have found in this book to work for you. Use it how you want to! Do it. I've come up with a Top 10 list for you to continue to grow, to parent, to live by as you go about your life. Although it's the last chapter in this book, it is in no way the previous chapter for you! Just in raising your child, your life will undoubtedly go through ups and downs, challenges, and victories. I look forward to meeting you and hearing about your journey.

ABOUT THE AUTHOR

Deanna Jones is a speaker and trainer from Columbus, Ohio. Deanna uses her professional and personal experience to empower those around her. By helping to cultivate hope and operate in resilience Deanna has empowered hundreds of individuals achieve their goal. By the time Deanna was 18 she had aged out of foster care with two small children in tow and no help. Deanna sought to defy the statistical failure that was sure to beset her by doing then what she teaches others now: deciding to have hope so that she could operate in resilience to achieve her goals. She did just that! Deanna is now the co-owner of Regal Beauty, a hair and beauty supply store in Columbus, Ohio and owner of Deanna J. Speaks! Through Deanna J. Speaks Deanna engages in speaking, training and life coaching. She is the mother of three children and a die-hard HGTV enthusiast.

facebook.com/deanna.jones.75685

instagram.com/deannajspeaks

Made in the USA
Columbia, SC
19 October 2022

69725262R00063